Communicating Knowledge Visually

Will Burtin
Scientific Information Design

Communicating Knowledge Visually

Will Burtin's Scientific Approach to Information Design

R. Roger Remington
Sheila Pontis, Ph.D.

Communicating Knowledge Visually

Will Burtin's Scientific Approach to Information Design

Published and distributed by:

RIT | RIT Press

RIT Press
90 Lomb Memorial Drive
Rochester, New York 14623
http://ritpress.rit.edu

ISBN 978-1-939125-85-9 (print)
ISBN 97810939125-86-6 (e-book)

Designed by Bruce Ian Meader
Printed in the USA

Library of Congress Cataloging-in-Publication Data

Names
Remington, R. Roger, author.
Pontis, Sheila, author.

Title
Communicating Knowledge Visually:
Will Burtin's Scientific Approach to Information Design
R. Roger Remington, Sheila Victoria Pontis, Ph.D.

Description
Rochester, New York: RIT Press, [2021]
Includes bibliographical references and index.

Summary
"Communicating Knowledge Visually: Will Burtin's Scientific Approach to Information Design presents an in-depth examination of the work of German designer Will Burtin, by introducing him as a true pioneer in his approach to information design. Burtin's innovative theories emphasized making conceptual design decisions informed by research to develop a strong foundation and discover effective solutions. Colorfully illustrated with step-by-step descriptions of nine seminal projects, the book provides a thorough analysis of his scientific approach to information design."
Provided by publisher.

Identifiers
LCCN 2021002585 (print)
LCCN 2021002586 (ebook)
ISBN 9781939125859 (softcover)
ISBN 9781939125866 (ebook)

Subjects
LCSH: Burtin, Will, 1908–1972–Criticism and interpretation.
Commercial art–United States–History–20th century.
Graphic arts–United States–History–20th century.

Classification
LCC NC999.4.B87 R458 2021 (print)
LCC NC999.4.B87 (ebook)
DDC 741.6092–dc23
LC record available at https://lccn.loc.gov/2021002585
LC ebook record available at https://lccn.loc.gov/2021002586

DEDICATION

To M. Suzanne Remington
and Horacio G. Pontis
without whose inspiration and support
this book never would have happened

Communicating Knowledge Visually

Will Burtin's Scientific Approach to Information Design

Table of Contents

Table of Contents

Top
Image 0
Small-scale model for exhibition for
Brunswick Corporation in Chicago, 1965.

Will Burtin: Triumph of the Will

Steven Heller
American Art Director

Despite a rise in the number of archives, exhibitions and monographs dedicated to the graphic and information designers who decades earlier had made impressive inroads in the field, it is surprising that there is a lack of knowledge about the collective professional design heritage.
Many of design's legacy figures, whose accomplishments should be familiar to design students, professionals and researchers, have slipped through the cracks because graphic design history is stalled. Suffice to say, there are many new kinds of histories that have yet to be explored.

Essential to the development of any foundational graphic and information design history, "form-givers" and "influencers" must be known by more than their names. Teams, movements and schools must be contextualized within the political, cultural and technological histories of their times.
R. Roger Remington and Sheila Pontis's book is about one person who deserves a share of attention: Will Burtin.
His approach to visualizing knowledge was "grounded in his lifelong career focus on combining convenience, clarity, usability, timeliness, [and] beauty." He began around the same time that Czech émigré designer, Ladislav Sutnar, introduced an archetypal information-heavy navigational system for industrial and product catalogs (for the Sweets Catalog Service) through distinct typographic hierarchies and easy-to-use grids. Burtin helped pioneer what has become known as information design in the sciences and technology, and in particular, devised advanced visual methods for clarifying otherwise densely presented theorems, postulates and other intellectual platforms. As an art director for the magazines *Fortune* and *SCOPE* (the in-house periodical for Upjohn pharmaceuticals), Burtin employed an artist's eye with a scientific fluency to create two- and three-dimensional graphics and typographic based exhibitions that increased data fluency and popular comprehension of healthcare, finance, industry and science. His most reputed work, a walk-through display of the human cell, introduced viewers to a magnified microscopic universe as larger than life, unforgettable environment. This had a significant influence on designers entering this now large practice.

Born in 1908 Cologne, Germany, Will Burtin apprenticed and became an exhibition and graphic designer during the postwar mid-1920s. Despite economic deprivations and political uncertainties stemming from military defeat, Germany's Weimar Republic experienced a brief period of economic growth that triggered a wave of progressive/modern *Gebrauchsgraphikers* (commercial artists). Art and culture were also reaching an apex of an Avant Garde ascent. Experimentation spilled into commercial printing, advertising, graphic design and typography. The 1920s was a great age for designers–and for Burtin.

For Burtin, design was not just a service, it was a mission. Rooted in mathematically precise organization and artful aesthetics, he effortlessly thinned out the thickest data forests while spotlighting meaning. He made what the authors call "facts of the world" easier to understand and comprehend, thus informing action. Burtin believed that good design was a curative for the chaos of the cataclysmic European war. Through "process boxes", Remington and Pontis recreate the unique systematic approach that Burtin used to structure his graphic outcomes. What distinguishes this book from many design monographs, aside from the specific case studies, is the publication, for the first time, of firsthand accounts of his ideas and theories, and the positioning of those ideas to contribute to current design areas. The last three chapters put Burtin's legacy in context by illustrating how his design approach, effectively used in the past, can be used to address contemporary design issues in practice and education.

Burtin's earliest work involved design for industry, social welfare and education. Modernity was influenced by new technologies that promised a better future–or the illusion of one. This is the bedrock on which *Entwürfe Bürtin* (Designs by Burtin) built its reputation. In 1938, Will and Hilde Burtin fled Germany for the United States, where his innovations were enthusiastically embraced for his intellectual gift for imagining complex data in simplified visual forms.

This book by R. Roger Remington and Sheila Pontis, preceded in 2007 by Remington's and Robert S.P. Fripp's splendid *Design and Science: The Life and World of Will Burtin*, dives even deeper into Burtin's essential role in visualizing science, which today is the cornerstone of a significant *information design practice* concerned with making more accessible and revealing rarified information to a wider segment of the larger world.

Image 1.1
Will Burtin as a visiting
instructor at Black Mountain
College, photographed by his
wife, Hilde Burtin, 1946.

Introduction

1.1
A Designer Ahead of his Time

Will Burtin was a designer ahead of his time, and should have a prominent place in design history. However, his genius has been largely overlooked by industry leaders, current practitioners and design educators. Asked to name a few well-known 20th-century designers, today's design practitioners would likely mention Saul Bass, Charles and Ray Eames, Milton Glaser, William Golden, Paul Rand, Stefan Sagmeister and Ladislav Sutnar; but only a few would name Burtin, despite his outstanding 40-plus-year career as an art director, graphic designer, exhibition director, educator and consultant. What made Burtin stand out was his logical and functional approach to design, which stood in contrast to other designers of his time. Today, Burtin's approach would be described as that of an *information designer*, a term used to describe the design practice aimed at facilitating understanding. His work focused on explaining rather than simply creating persuasive or aesthetically pleasing solutions. Like information design itself, Burtin's work emphasized clear communication and functionality.

R. Roger Remington has written extensively about Burtin's work and contributions: *Nine Pioneers in American Graphic Design*, with Barbara Hodik (1989); *Design and Science: The Life and Work of Will Burtin*, with Burtin's son-in-law, Robert S. P. Fripp (2007); and an RIT Press Chapbook, *Will Burtin: The Display of Visual Knowledge* (2009). The first book presents a small selection of Burtin's work; the second describes his life, projects and achievements; and the third offers a summary of his career. None, however, look at Burtin's projects in depth, analyze his design process or show how his accomplishments have the potential to both inform and impact current information design practice and education. This book attempts to fill that gap by presenting Burtin's projects in more detail, with an emphasis on his innovative design process and philosophy, and an analysis through an information design lens. It also highlights the potential impact and influence that his work and ideas might have on contemporary information design practice and education.

Image 1.2
Will Burtin in Fire Island, on
the beach, photographed by
his wife, Hilde Burtin, c. 1947.

1.2
The Importance of Information Design Today

Information design prioritizes shaping content into functional and rational forms rather than strictly aesthetic expression. Complex, unknown or disorganized information is presented structurally in a way that fosters competence and understanding. Information designers shape the "facts of the world" to enhance knowledge, facilitate comprehension and inform action. Information design solutions must advance understanding. Edward Tufte, Richard Saul Wurman, Joel Katz, Sandra Rendgen, Jorge Frascara and many others have written extensively on information design, using terms such as "visualization," "information architecture," "communication design" and "visual explanation design" to describe this type of work.

Scientists and businessmen alike have found that information design can help clarify complex messages, making them more accessible to wider audiences. Communicating complexity is challenging, information architect Wurman explains, but can also be "wonderfully sophisticated and rich—even dense, textured and beautiful–as long as it is understandable."[1] Burtin's primary goal, like that of many information designers, was to explain complex, technical information–such as scientific, medical or military concepts–and make it accessible to both expert and lay audiences.

Re-examining Burtin's work through an information design lens is extremely timely due to a growing interest in tapping the field's full potential and recognizing its value.[2] This interest reflects how difficult it is to make sense of what is being manufactured at the same pace as it is being produced.

1.3
Will Burtin's Journey to Information Design

Burtin began his graphic design career in Cologne, Germany, as an apprentice in a typography shop. He was greatly influenced by European avant-garde designers and artists before emigrating to the United States in 1938. During the first part of the 20th century, most designers worked as commercial artists creating posters, advertisements and branding.

However, early in his career, Burtin drew upon his basic graphic design skills to instead focus on explaining and visualizing scientific content,[3] which made him stand out from other designers. He referred to this type of work as "Visual Communications"[4] to distinguish it from work in advertising or branding. Burtin "made scientific knowledge visible."[5] He worked to organize and communicate the essential aspects of "invisible phenomena" that are "too big, too small, too slow or too abstract for normal sensory comprehension."[6] He explained scientific content through visualizations, augmenting or decreasing scales as needed, and invited experts and lay audiences on a journey in which the complex and unknown became coherent, informative and comprehensible.

Burtin's design process was distinctive because he followed a scientific approach, uncommon among designers at the time. As part of his analytical and systematic approach, Burtin believed in doing extensive research on the subject of each project. Rather than working with illustrative languages and popular graphic forms, he combined graphic clarity and directness to fashion a clear, understandable presentation of the subject matter.[7] Burtin described his approach to design as integrating visuals and content in response to people's needs that he had identified through research. His process started by interviewing subject-matter experts or immersing himself firsthand in the experience he needed to explain to gain familiarity with it and thoroughly understand it. He then made design decisions based on that understanding rather than on his prior experience, which freed him from relying on subjectivity and the accidental.

Burtin's design career in America included stints as a graphic designer, exhibition designer, editorial art director and consultant for prominent clients such as the US Army and the Upjohn Company, one of America's leading pharmaceutical companies. In all of his work, he valued design as the vehicle to communicate messages to the intended audience.

1.4
A Need for Understanding

An increased need to understand the world has long been a calling for designers, and particularly information designers, who yearn to make complex information more accessible.[8] The goal of this book is to emphasize the value of information design and the search for "...its identity and its boundaries"[9] by examining Burtin's scientific approach to visualizing complex information.

Educator Paul A. Miller stated, "How journeys begin and continue through twists in the road yield stories to be remembered and perhaps told."[10] We believe that Will Burtin's story should be remembered and told. We explore his journey to make complex information more understandable and explain how it emerged and developed. Burtin was a pioneer of information design, and his process, way of working and accomplishments have much to offer to today's information design students and professionals.

This book provides a thorough analysis of Burtin's work and his approach to information design.

- We examine Burtin's work using seven dimensions of information design that represent continuing themes of debate in design professional practice and education.
- We discuss Burtin's scientific approach to design and his information design mindset, which emphasizes making conceptual design decisions informed by research to develop a strong foundation and effective solutions.
- We explore the steps necessary for the translation of complex information into more accessible forms using Burtin's design process as a framework. The term *information designer* did not exist in Burtin's lifetime but, nevertheless, his design process can be used to understand how today's information design professionals can and should think. We also include step-by-step descriptions of Burtin's process followed to complete some of the projects–called Process Boxes–to illustrate core information design challenges, tasks, and activities.
- To showcase Burtin's relevance to the current field of information design, we highlight the parallels between the types of challenges that Burtin faced in his time and those that designers encounter today.

- We explain how Burtin's approach to design can address those challenges and equip today's information designers with a more scientific design mindset to deal with complex problems.
- We examine Burtin's innovative theories and ideas that can give today's information design educators the tools they need to teach design with a scientific approach.

This book has been written for (1) design students, who will benefit from the educational approach and design process guidance; (2) practicing designers, who will find meaning and inspiration in the approach presented; (3) scientists, who will be inspired by Burtin's innovative approaches to scientific topics; and (4) people involved in public education, communications and scientific outreach, especially those who create museum and other educational exhibitions designed to make science more accessible to lay audiences.

The book has two parts.

Part One

This part (Chapters 2 and 3) introduces the main character and core concepts analyzed in the book: Will Burtin, information design, and Burtin's scientific approach to design. Chapter 2 includes a biography of Burtin, based on interviews and email correspondence with his daughter, Carol Burtin Fripp, and a description of his major influences in a historical context. Chapter 3 introduces and explains information design, its process and key principles, and describes Burtin's scientific approach.

Part Two

This part (Chapters 4 through 10) presents Burtin's approach to design in action through the examination of his work housed in the Will Burtin Collection at the Cary Graphic Design Archive at Rochester Institute of Technology (RIT), NY. Many of these projects have never been exhibited or written about before. Using his own words, these chapters examine what it meant for Burtin to make sense of a complex subject through nine of his seminal projects, each project also representing a dimension of information design:

- *Metabolism, the Cycle of Life* exhibition
  (Chapter 4: Purpose)
- *The Brain* exhibition (Chapter 5: Problem)
- *Gunner's Information File* project
  (Chapter 6: Audience)
- *The Cell* exhibition (Chapter 7: Approach)
- *Fortune* and *SCOPE* magazines (Chapter 8: Outcome)
- *Visual Aspects of Science* and *The Communication of Knowledge* exhibitions (Chapter 9: Practice)
- Burtin's ideas on design education and
  The Story of Mathematics for Young People book
  (Chapter 10: Education).

The resulting artifacts from the showcased projects are shown with great granularity. Five of the projects feature a Process Box with Burtin's own words highlighting his forward-thinking ideas. Chapter 10 also provides suggestions to rethink information design education through a scientific lens informed by Burtin's ideas and theories. The book concludes with Chapter 11, which recommends means to help improve information design based on lessons learned from both Burtin's experience and a critical examination of his work.

NOTES

1 Richard S. Wurman, "Hats," *Design Quarterly* 145 (1989): 1–32: 5.

2 Wurman, "Hats"; Inge Gobert and Johan Van Looveren, *Thoughts on Designing Information* (Zurich, Switzerland: Lars Müller, 2014).

3 Philip B. Meggs, *A History of Graphic Design*, 3rd ed. (New York: John Wiley, 1998), 315.

4 Will Burtin to Dean Christ-Janier, The Art School, Pratt Institute, "Memorandum on the Organization of a Design Department which Teaches 'Visual Communications,'" circa 1959, Will Burtin Papers, 96.9–97.3 (box 17: folder 3 of 8), Cary Graphic Design Archive, RIT.

5 Meggs, *History*, 315.

6 Eric Siegel, "Too Big, Too Small, Too Slow, Too Abstract: Exhibiting Modern Science," *Exhibitionist* 27, no. 2 (Fall 2008): 22, https://static1.squarespace.com/static/58fa260a725e25c 4f30020f3/t/59499b72f7e0abeec2b950b4/1497996195827/6+ EXH_fall08_Too+Big+Too+Small+Too+Slow+Too+Abstract-Exhibiting+Modern+Science_Siegel_Baker_Martin.pdf.

7 Meggs, *History*.

8 Steven Heller and Rick Landers, *Infographic Designers' Sketchbooks* (New York: Princeton Architectural Press, 2014); Jorge Frascara, *Information Design as Principled Action: Making Information Accessible, Relevant, Understandable, and Usable* (Champaign, IL: Common Ground, 2015).

9 Gobert and van Looveren, *Thoughts*, 154.

10 Paul A. Miller, *Bridging Campus and Community: Events, Excerpts, and Expectations for Strengthening America's Collaborative Competence: A Professional Memoir* (Self-published, 2014), 297.

Image 2.1
Will Burtin in Lake Como, on a holiday
cruise, photographed by his wife,
Hilde Burtin, c. 1932.

An Overview of Will Burtin's Life

2.1
Beginnings on the Rhine

At the turn of the last century, Cologne, Germany was known as a vibrant cultural center. Will Burtin was born in Köln-Ehrenfeld, on the outskirts of Cologne, on January 27, 1908, to August and Gertrud Bürtin. Köln-Ehrenfeld was an industrial area, unlike the more sophisticated central city near the Kölner-Dom, Cologne's majestic cathedral. Burtin's father was a glassblower for the chemical laboratory in a tire and rubber factory.

Burtin grew up in a religious family. He was an altar boy at Gereonskirche,[1] a Roman Catholic church in Cologne, which meant that on weekdays, he often walked to church at 5 o'clock in the morning, lit candles and served Mass and then continued on to school. This experience taught him the communicative power of images and developed his sensitivity for symbols:

> Cold and bored, he had been gazing around Gereonskirche when he had his moment of epiphany. Church illustration, intended to school the illiterate, speaks without text. There is much in Burtin's work– in exhibitions and print–to suggest that he drew on lessons learned from iconography. These were both positive (the power of image to communicate) and negative (his penchant for avoiding visual clutter came to include dislike for serif fonts). ... His brilliance as a visual communicator began with those frigid mornings in Gereonskirche.[2]

Burtin's formal education was disrupted during the First World War when his school was taken over by the state to become a hospital. This event left him with a powerful, lifelong desire to learn, and as a result, he placed a high priority on comprehension in every design project he undertook. Throughout his life, Burtin was passionate about investigating scientific subjects like bacteriology, which have been known to confuse other designers.[3] Later in his career, Burtin could frequently be found in the "rare books" sections of libraries, such as that of the New York Public Library. His lack of a formal education encouraged Burtin to develop a more creative mind, and his own ways of approaching problem solving, which were different from those taught in Art and Design schools at the time.[4]

One of the great ironies in Burtin's life was that, while his formal learning ended abruptly during his eighth grade school year, he went on to work with many of the most renowned designers, physicians and scientists of his time. Both his indefatigable curiosity and his hunger for learning helped him develop a strong commitment to whatever work he chose to do. These attributes were at the core of Burtin's quest to make information clear and understandable through visual means.

2.2
A Graphic Designer of German Precision

In 1922, 14-year-old Burtin began a challenging four-year apprenticeship in typesetting at a local letterpress shop, *Handwerkskammer zu Köln* (Chamber of Crafts in Cologne). This experience provided the context for his professional career, for it was an environment that demanded exactitude, logic and pragmatism. He had to think systematically as he shaped messages and images into clear, functional designs. The shop was a technical world of vertical and horizontal alignment.

During and following his apprenticeship, Burtin also worked in another type shop, operated by Dr. Philippe Knöll, who became an important mentor. Knöll insisted that Burtin, in order to broaden his visual vocabulary, concurrently take courses at the *Kölner Werkschulen* (Cologne Art and Craft Schools). These classes introduced Burtin to the larger, expressive world of graphic design.

In 1926, the *International Hygiene* exhibition, *GeSoLei* (*Gesundheitspflege, soziale Fürsorge und Leibesübungen*) was held in Düsseldorf. The fair emphasized healthcare, social welfare and physical exercise and brought much work to Burtin in terms of typesetting and graphic design. Helping to meet the communication needs of an event of this magnitude and scale deeply shaped Burtin's ideas about working in graphics and exhibition design.

Burtin opened his own design studio in Cologne in 1927, where he created brochures, posters, type books, exhibition materials, displays and advertising. At the same time, his interest in learning and education encouraged him to teach design part-time at the *Kölner Werkschulen*. In 1932, he married one of his students, Hilde Munk, who became a partner in their firm, *Entwürfe Bürtin* (Designs by Burtin). Hilde greatly enhanced the work of the studio by contributing her photography skills to the enterprise–photography was rapidly replacing illustration as the preferred imaging format in graphic design.

2.3
Modernism in the Air

For the young professional designers, the 1920s were heady times. All over Europe, designers were moving toward a new aesthetic that stressed functionalism and the integration of word and image.[5] Despite a serious economic depression, designers were embracing the avant-garde reaction to the Victorian era, breaking boundaries for the creative arts (as was also happening in painting, sculpture, music, photography, architecture, literature and dance). In Europe, this new way of thinking was *in the air*. Burtin was surrounded by a spirit of innovation, which had a profound effect on his development as a designer and on his design practice.

Germany was the locus of many of these creative avant-garde innovations and became a cultural hub. New ideas in the arts poured in from other European countries. German designer Jan Tschichold's asymmetrical page organization became a significant influence on designers. He published his ideas on typography in a groundbreaking book, *Die Neue Typographie* (The New Typography), published in Berlin in 1928. After this, the *Ring Neue Werbegestalter* group (Circle of New Advertising Designers) came together under the leadership of Kurt Schwitters to promote a common typographic vision. László Moholy-Nagy, a Hungarian artist, was also involved in bringing this group into existence, and other key group members were Willi Baumeister, Max Burchartz, Walter Dexel, César Domela and Piet Zwart. The group members shared their progressive ideas, and organized exhibitions showcasing their work. The graphic style of these designers was characterized by the exclusive use of sans serif type, especially Futura, designed by Paul Renner in 1927. Kurt Schwitters and others began combining lines of type, graphical symbols and other elements in vertical and diagonal directions across the page.

The *Staatliches Bauhaus*, a German art school active between 1919 and 1933 and commonly known simply as the Bauhaus, became a central point of experimentation in art, design and crafts education. Founded with the idea that there would be a unification of the arts, the school became famous for its rational and functional approach to design. Especially in the graphic work of Herbert Bayer, Joost Schmidt and Josef Albers, the Bauhaus style was one of the most influential in Modernist design. The Bauhaus, particularly in its Dessau period, 1925–1932, had a profound influence upon developments in all the major design fields.

Other areas of Europe produced design innovations as well. Russian Constructivist artist and designer El Lissitzky traveled around Europe spreading his progressive ideas about art and design, such as using page tabs to navigate through a book. For him, the new was never new enough. He visited the Bauhaus school and German printing facilities frequently, spreading his typographic ideas and constructivist visual style.[6] Czechoslovakian designer Ladislav Sutnar synthesized his avant-garde thinking before emigrating to the US. He became a master at integrating photography and type in book covers. And Filippo Marinetti led an Italian Futurist movement that forged its own dynamic typographic design style with the slogan, "Words in freedom."

In the midst of this zeitgeist, Burtin continued searching, learning and designing. His work during the 1920s and 1930s mirrored that of many of these European, avant-garde, experimental graphic designers. Like Lissitzky, who didn't "decorate" his designs but rather "visually programmed" them,[7] Burtin rejected traditional and decorative elements. His Modernist visual grammar emphasized simplicity and the direct communication of messages; for Burtin, the content of the message was primary. He practiced a rational, objective and systematic method of designing, using maps, symbols and diagrams as visual forms to synthesize meaning.

Burtin's brochures are examples of functional design that incorporates page tabs and graphic symbols to aid navigation. Shapes and colors are arranged to create visual unity throughout the pages. The organization of elements on the page is asymmetrical, a grid system making everything consistent and legible. Overall, Burtin implemented a coherent visual hierarchy in terms of the total effect of the visual syntax on the intended communication.

His design style can be seen in the *Kristall-Spiegelglas* (Crystal Mirror Glass) brochure that Burtin designed in 1932 to promote industrial glass. (see images 2.2 to 2.9.) The brochure had two covers: a clear acetate sheet with one red word in the middle; and the titles of the four sections on the right side, followed by a page of black cardstock printed in white ink. The four sections of the brochure were distinguished with numbered, clear acetate sheets for each of the cover titles: (1) *Die Herstellung* (Manufacturing); (2) *Die Vorzüge* (Benefits); (3) *Die Verwendung* (Use); and (4) *Die Preise* (Prices). The interior pages combined text with full-page images created using photo montages, illustrations and diagrams. The brochure was small in size (8 × 6 in.) and pages but was extremely rich conceptually and graphically.

Images 2.2 and 2.3
Front (right) and back covers, *Kristall-Spiegelglas* brochure, 1932.

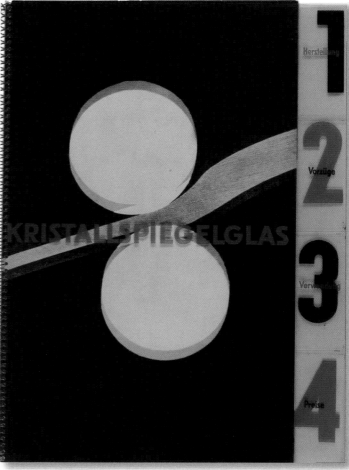

Image 2.4
Table of contents, *Kristall-Spiegelglas* brochure.

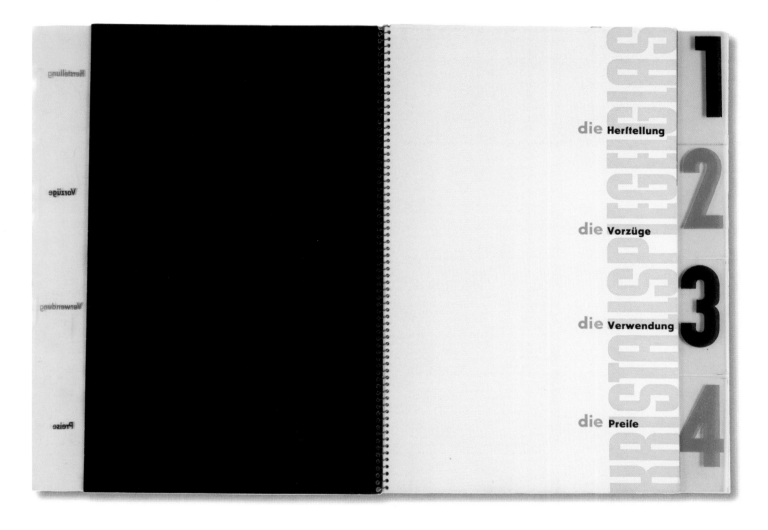

Image 2.5
Opening pages, *Kristall-Spiegelglas* brochure.

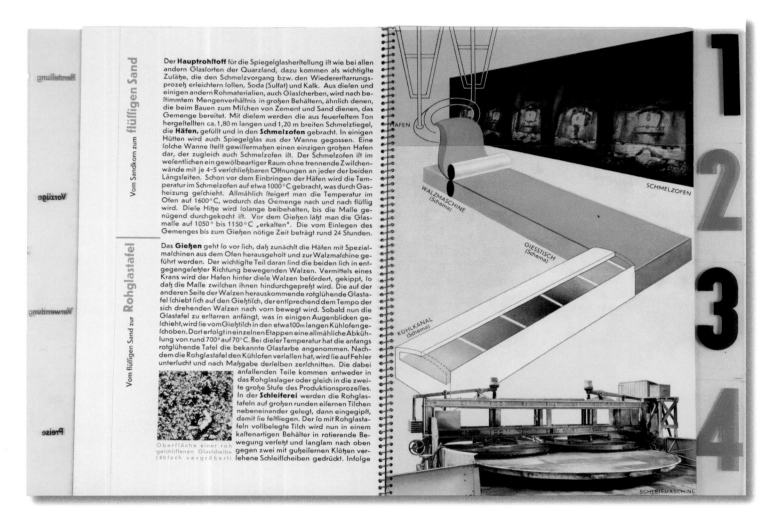

Image 2.6
Opening pages, *Kristall-Spiegelglas* brochure.

Image 2.7
Inside pages, *Kristall-Spielgelglas* brochure.

Image 2.8
Inside pages, *Kristall-Spielgelglas* brochure.

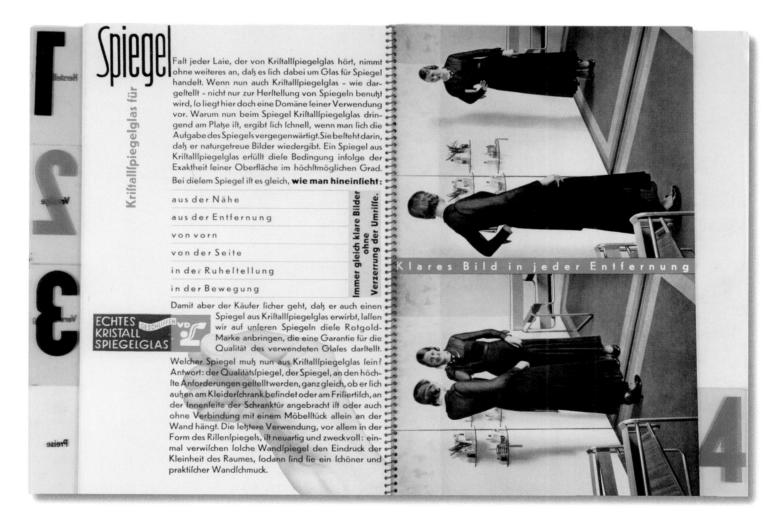

Image 2.9
Inside pages, *Kristall-Spielgelglas* brochure.

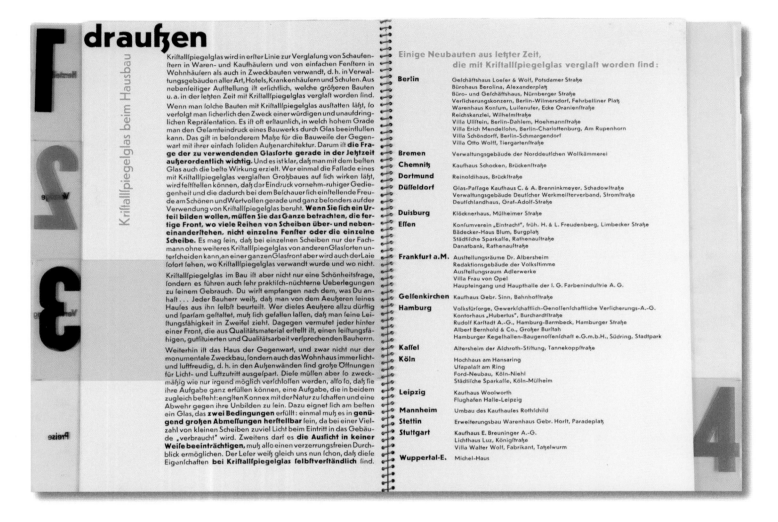

Image 2.10
Will and Hilde Burtin
on a holiday cruise, c. 1932.

The *Kristall-Spiegelglas* brochure unquestionably shows the influence that the Bauhaus and Lissitzky had on Burtin. Throughout his career, Burtin continued to apply a functional rationale for designing printed matter and exhibitions, similar to that of the Bauhaus designers who had developed the style for building houses.

Burtin later summarized the influence that these avant-garde movements and individuals had on him:

> The painters of the cubist, constructivist, dadaist and suprematist schools, the new architecture, photography and the great feats of technology supported my growing awareness of connections between what I was doing in the composing room with the changes taking place in the world around me–meaning Europe.

> The new typography thus reflected the complete upheaval of the values and traditions upon which European thought had rested up to that time. Even language underwent such transitions as to change the very meaning of words. It had become the function of the typographer to help define words through emphasis, grouping, choice of typefaces, color and the organization of space. Presenting the first clear formulation of these design principles is the historic achievement of the revolutionaries of the Twenties.[8]

Burtin's commercial work of this period shows equal care for function and form, integrating organically the visual variables of the avant-garde and his sensitivity to the changing creative environment in Europe. At the same time, these influences evidenced the beginning of a shift in his career; he was developing a scientific approach to design.

2.4
An Émigré Mind

Will Burtin achieved prominent status in Germany while in his twenties and might have remained among the leaders of European graphic and typographic avant-garde if the rise of the Nazi Party had not intervened. But the department store owned by Hilde Munk's father, Ernst, was taken over by the Nazis, and everything changed.

The Nazi Party's success was due to many factors, but propaganda was a primary cause.[9] Propaganda was used to spread the Party's ideas through simple slogans and messages to maximize their reach across the public. Because of Burtin's growing reputation as a designer in Germany, it was not long before his designs were brought to the attention of the Nazi Party and he was moved to the top of the list of possible designers to be recruited. Nazi officials began pressuring Burtin to design for them and he was repeatedly asked to come on board.[10] They wanted his design work for the Thousand-Year Reich (Germany's official name until 1945) to stand beside Leni Riefenstahl's iconic film work. Burtin confided to his daughter Carol that, in 1937, Nazi Propaganda Minister Joseph Goebbels formally asked him to become the director of design for the Ministry.[11]

Politically, the Burtins were Liberal or Social Democrats and very anti-Nazi. Beyond their political views, the situation was more critical because Burtin's wife Hilde was Jewish. Already by the mid 1930s, both families had been victims of the Nazis[12] and they would not work for them. Hence, it was necessary for them to leave Germany. While Burtin managed to put off the repeated requests, Hilde asked her cousin, Dr. Max Munk of Maryland, to sponsor them so that they could move to the US. Shortly after receiving an affidavit from the American government granting them visas, Burtin received a request to travel to Berlin for a meeting with Adolf Hitler. Because another refusal to join the Nazis would be open to investigation, Burtin had to change his strategy. During the meeting, Burtin requested time to transition, since he had so much work in his studio that needed to be completed. He also asked for some additional time for a holiday with his wife between positions. Hitler agreed.

By the time Burtin arrived home from Berlin, Hilde had already packed their bags. They left their home and boarded the steamship Statendam in Rotterdam, bound for America. On July 13, 1938, they arrived in New York and were met at the dock by Dr. Munk and other family relatives. The Munk family helped the Burtins become established in their new country.

2.5
A Fresh Career in America
The international German design journal *Gebrauchsgraphik* (Commercial Graphics) "published some of the first reviews of an activity still to be termed 'graphic design,' together with articles on book design, advertising, publicity and packaging,"[13] and had featured Burtin's design work. As a result of this and articles about him in other publications, he was already well-known in the American design and advertising communities. Burtin's reputation made his transition to the New York design world much easier.

Many immigrant designers, used to the rich history of European design, pictured the design scene in America as being undeveloped, crude and even a "blank slate." Burtin, however, was pleasantly surprised: "In the US I found conditions which made the continuation of studies possible: people less biased by narrow interpretations of tradition; devotion to high productivity; a great industrial apparatus."[14] Burtin had found much room for building a new design career.

With family help and supportive professional contacts such as Dr. Robert Leslie at The Composing Room, Inc., Burtin's career soon flourished in New York. He designed exhibitions for the New York World's Fair in 1939; produced print materials for the Upjohn Pharmaceutical Company; designed covers for *The Architectural Forum* magazine; and, after entering the military, worked for the US Army designing Air Force instructional manuals. Burtin also taught graphic design courses to undergraduates at Pratt Institute: "I taught them design; they taught me English."[15]

Will and Hilde's only child, Carol, was born in 1942. As the War years were winding down, America experienced a dynamic revitalization in business and industry. The factories and industries that had been marshalled for America's "arsenal of democracy" were now available for consumer goods and more. In the mid 1940s, *Fortune*, America's premier business magazine with a circulation in 1937 of around 460,000,[16] was searching for a new Art Director. Burtin had worked as advisor and designer for *TIME*, *LIFE*, *The Architectural Forum* and *Fortune* before he went into the Army in 1943, and was therefore a known entity to magazine editors. He had had more than 20 years of experience in the design field, and was well versed in scientific, industrial, economic, geographic and social topics. These qualities made Burtin a strong candidate, not unnoticed by *Fortune*'s managers. In 1945, *Fortune* approached the military to ask that Burtin be released from his service commitment to serve "the national interest" in a different way, by leading the magazine in these demanding new economic times. *Fortune*'s managers explained to the Army that Will Burtin was "without question the man best fitted for the position."[17] The Army agreed, Burtin accepted the position, and he worked as art director of *Fortune* magazine from 1945 to 1949.

Following his time with *Fortune*, Burtin opened his own design firm in New York. In 1949, Burtin became the chief designer for Upjohn Pharmaceuticals in Kalamazoo, Michigan. Upjohn became his major career client and he continued working there until his death in 1971.

Hilde Burtin passed away in 1960, and roughly one year later, Burtin married designer Cipe Pineles, who had been a close family friend. Pineles was the widow of graphic designer William Golden, who had died in 1959. She was one of the few prominent women designers of her time, working as art director for *Seventeen* and *Glamour* magazines.

Burtin's mature years of designing graphic and exhibition installations for Upjohn gave him the chance to develop innovative ways of explaining complex content. In this pioneering work, Burtin bridged the fields of design and science, becoming one of the first graphic designers to employ an information design mindset. His approach and strategies for design work will be further explained in the following chapters.

Left to right
Image 2.11
Will Burtin and his daughter, Carol,
photographed by his wife, Hilde Burtin, 1948.

Image 2.12
Will Burtin and his wife, Cipe Pineles,
discussing a new design, 1962.

NOTES

1 In Germany, Gereonskirchen are churches
  dedicated to their patron, Saint Gereon of Cologne.

2 R. Roger Remington and Robert S. P. Fripp,
  Design and Science: The Life and Work of Will Burtin
  (Hampshire, UK: Lund Humphries, 2007), 30.

3 Philip B. Meggs, *A History of Graphic Design*, 3rd ed.
  (New York: John Wiley, 1998).

4 Alex F. Osborn, *Applied Imagination:
  Principles and Procedures of Creative Problem-Solving*, rev. ed.
  (Buffalo, NY: Creative Education Foundation, 1993).

5 Meggs, *History*.

6 Ibid.

7 Ibid, 265.

8 Will Burtin, "From Where to Where?" in *Typography–
  USA Forum: 'What is New in American Typography?'
  April 18, 1959, Hotel Biltmore, New York City*
  (New York: Type Directors Club of New York, 1959), 5,
  Cary Graphic Arts Collection, 106609, SRIT

9 BBC Bitesize. Why the Nazis achieved power.
  BBC [Online] Available at:
  https://www.bbc.co.uk/bitesize/guides/zsrwjxs/revision/7

10 Meggs, *History*.

11 Carol Burtin Fripp and Robert Fripp, in discussion
  with the authors, September 30, 2001, Rochester, NY.

12 "If you are asking for their political views in the 1930s,
  before they escaped, I'm guessing they would have been
  Liberal or Social Democrats, very anti- Nazi. Also, do not forget
  that already in the mid-1930s some of my mother's cousins
  had been arrested and disappeared, and her father was losing
  his department store in Osterode to the new Nazi policy of
  taking control of all Jewish-owned businesses... Furthermore,
  my father's youngest sister Christa, who was disabled,
  was killed when the Nazis shot patients in hospitals who were
  not going to recover.... she of course was Catholic, as was the
  Burtin family." Carol Burtin Fripp, in email correspondence with
  the authors, September 18, 2020.

13 Jeremy Aynsley, "'Gebrauchsgraphik' as an Early Graphic Design
  Journal, 1924–1938," *Journal of Design History* 5, no. 1 (1992): 53.

14 Burtin, *Integration–The New Discipline in Design*,
  exhibition brochure (Chicago: Art Directors Club, 1949),
  Will Burtin Papers, 55.6 and 90.12–90.13,
  Cary Graphic Design Archive, RIT.

15 Remington and Fripp, *Design*, 30.

16 Laura Massey, "Fortune," *Peter Harrington London*
  (December 11, 2010),
  http://www.peterharrington.co.uk/blog/fortune/

17 Remington and Fripp, *Design*, 39.

Diagram 3.1
Dimensions of information design including
Will Burtin's projects relevant to each.

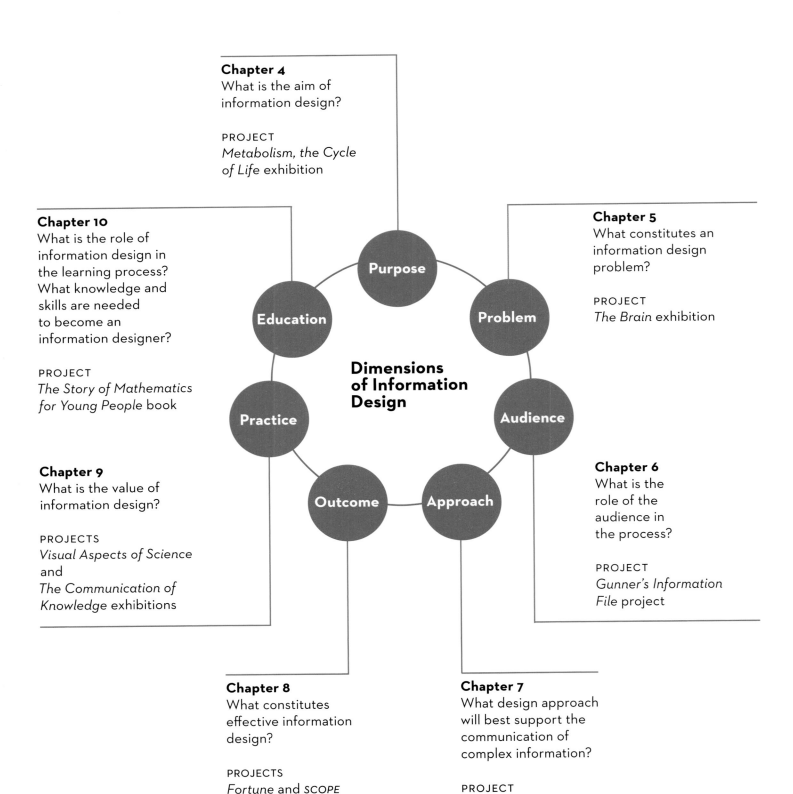

Chapter 4
What is the aim of
information design?

PROJECT
*Metabolism, the Cycle
of Life* exhibition

Chapter 10
What is the role of
information design in
the learning process?
What knowledge and
skills are needed
to become an
information designer?

PROJECT
*The Story of Mathematics
for Young People* book

Chapter 9
What is the value of
information design?

PROJECTS
Visual Aspects of Science
and
*The Communication of
Knowledge* exhibitions

Chapter 5
What constitutes an
information design
problem?

PROJECT
The Brain exhibition

Chapter 6
What is the
role of the
audience in
the process?

PROJECT
*Gunner's Information
File* project

Purpose

Education

Problem

**Dimensions
of Information
Design**

Practice

Audience

Outcome

Approach

Chapter 8
What constitutes
effective information
design?

PROJECTS
Fortune and *SCOPE*
magazines

Chapter 7
What design approach
will best support the
communication of
complex information?

PROJECT
The Cell exhibition

A Designer with an Information Priority

Most of Burtin's work while living in the US involved translating military tasks and cutting-edge scientific research in pharmacology, microbiology, biochemistry and nuclear physics into visual forms (such as publications, graphics and exhibitions) so that they would be easily understood by both experienced audiences (medical doctors, scientists, Air Force and Navy servicemen) and novice audiences (general public and students). He also taught design, and was active in organizing significant design conferences. Working on a variety of design projects challenged Burtin to broaden his understanding of the potential role of the designer. Although he intuitively applied information design principles to his work, his thinking, processes and skills evolved with each new project, as he became a designer focusing on enhancing communication.

3.1
Understanding, the Foundation

Throughout his practice and in his writings, Burtin fostered the emergence of a new design specialization called *Integration*. He described it as "a comprehensive and anticipatory activity... concerned with *all* problems of understanding."[1] This definition coincides with the core aim of contemporary information design as stated by various current authors, including Wurman,[2] Tufte,[3] Pettersson,[4] and Frascara[5]: to enhance understanding– of a situation, concept, space, place, time, quantity, phenomenon– for an intended audience.

Furthermore, information design is a multidisciplinary practice[6] aimed at helping people achieve their goals by translating raw data or disorganized content "into forms that can be rapidly perceived, understood, processed and used."[7] Information design draws from a range of academic disciplines related to making sense of and visually communicating content. These include graphic design, communication sciences, user experience design, cognitive science, perception, applied psychology, and information science and management.[8] Information design solutions encompass print, digital, environments, exhibitions, and experiences, but in all cases, the creation of visual forms or visualizations (e.g., diagrams, graphs, maps, 3D models) are an intrinsic component to translate and convey information.

The use of visualizations has long served as a means to help people understand the world.[9] Early examples date pre-cuneiform tablets at around 3,000 BC and the first cartographic maps were drawn in approximately 550 BC. Later examples of communicating complex concepts through visual forms were created by Leonardo da Vinci to illustrate his studies in science and engineering,[10] and more recent contributions include those from John Snow (regarding the cause of deaths from cholera in 1854),[11] Charles Minard (portraying the loss of life in Napoleon's 1812 Russian campaign),[12] Florence Nightingale (depicting mortality data from the Crimean War),[13] Sutnar (catalog design)[14] and Frank Netter (medical illustration).[15]

Today, computers have made the creation of digital visualizations common. However, in the 1940s and 1950s, Burtin was a pioneer in presenting scientific concepts in three-dimensional form as exhibitions[16] that encouraged understanding and visual reasoning. In 1948, Burtin and Lawrence Lessing, the writer for the text of Burtin's World War II wartime gunnery manuals, (see chapter 6) described visualization as "a form of visual reasoning whose purpose [was] to heighten and clarify man's understanding of the modern world."[17] They felt that visualizations were not "merely decorative" forms of art because they were "intimately connected with the needs of modern life."[18] Burtin believed that visualizations helped readers and viewers by stimulating their curiosity, making it easier for them to unravel complexity and thus rewarding them with new insight.[19]

The term "visualization" has many meanings and is associated with numerous disciplines ranging from computer science to psychology to graphic design. The 1966 edition of the *Random House Dictionary of the English Language* defines the aims of "visualizations" as making something "perceptible to the mind or imagination." In 1994, scientists James Foley and William Ribarsky at Georgia Institute of Technology suggested that visualization referred to "mapping" representations.[20] More current definitions state that visualization is "a tool or method for interpreting image data fed into a computer and for generating images from complex multi-dimensional data sets"[21] or, more simply put, a "graphical representation of data or concepts."[22] In general, visualizations allow people to process more content by distilling that content into a format that can be rapidly perceived and processed.[23] Harry Robin, author of *The Scientific Image: From Cave to Computer*, explains that when we look at visualizations, we transform "the static image into an active intellectual experience," potentially leading to new understanding.[24]

For our purposes, the term visualization is used in graphic and information design contexts. Visualizations are central to information design work today, as they were to Burtin's work, in order to make complexity more accessible. An information designer's process in making sense of and visualizing content involves a range of decisions, from determining what type of information is actually relevant and appropriate for a given audience to determining which tools, graphic techniques and formats to use.

3.2
Understanding the Information Design Process
Broadly speaking, the information design process comprises a series of steps and activities that an information designer performs in order to:

- make sense of a problem to be solved
- understand the intended audience
- find the hidden, inherent logic to explain the problem
- direct the audience's attention to that logic, to promote understanding and memory
- test the solution's effectiveness.

Unlike traditional graphic design, information design shifts the emphasis from the end of the process (prototype design) to the beginning of the process (conceptual design).[25]

During *conceptual design*, information designers start the activity of making sense of complexity or unorganized content by finding patterns and making associations, and then deciding what message to convey. Information design principles (which are "rooted both in findings about how people perceive and comprehend visual displays per se," and in "how our eyes and minds generally organize and interpret the world"[26]) help the designer to identify the excess information that needs to be removed, the pertinent information that should be retained and how this information should be presented to achieve clarity and understanding. (see images 3.1 to 3.5.)

Table 3.1
Five principles of effective information design.

	Principles of Effective Information Design	
1	Clear definition of problem	• Understand the problem • Dissect and reconstruct information • Learn about the audience's needs, struggles, understanding barriers, characteristics • Determine what message you want to convey • Make sure your audience understands the language, jargon, and concepts used
2	Well-defined hierarchies	• Find patterns, make connections and associations • Define structures to present the selected aspects of the information • Constructively synthesize information
3	Logical visual structure of the information	• Determine the most appropriate medium and format for the design solution (static/dynamic, print/digital, two-dimensional/three-dimensional, etc) • Define clear navigation and reading flow
4	Appropriate use of visual and textual language	• Learn about the target audience's needs, struggles, understanding barriers, characteristics • Make sure your audience understands the language, jargon, and concepts used • Use visuals that are related to the meaning • Anchor meaning of visuals with labels • Make the abstract tangible, and the unfamiliar familiar
5	Purposeful use of visual variables	• Clearly indicate differences using visual variables (color, shape, orientation, etc) • Distinguish two types of information using large enough visual proportions • Code related information with similar visual variables • Visually indicate priorities

The underlying logic of complex or unorganized content must be unraveled *before* (or in the process of) creating a solution.[27] Decisions made during this phase should be based on a deep understanding of a.) the problem to be solved, b.) the content, and c.) the intended audience, since this understanding will lead to ideas or proposals for potential solutions. The thoroughness of the decisions made at this point in the process will determine the quality and appropriateness of potential solutions. Once information designers generate a solution idea, they move into *prototype design*, where they will execute the idea and translate it into visualizations, thus creating the actual solutions[28]

The rigor of the analysis, the appropriateness of the organization of information, and, ultimately, the depth of understanding gained at each step of the process determine the success of the solution: "Its final test [is] in the understanding."[29] Achieving effective measurable results is also critical to the process. The quality of the results cannot be measured only according to technology or subjective aesthetic choices, but also through the intended audience's input.

Information Design Principles in Action

Image 3.1
Principle 1
Clear definition of problem.
Information graphic from *SCOPE* magazine indicating the
components involved in transplanting gut segment, 1955.

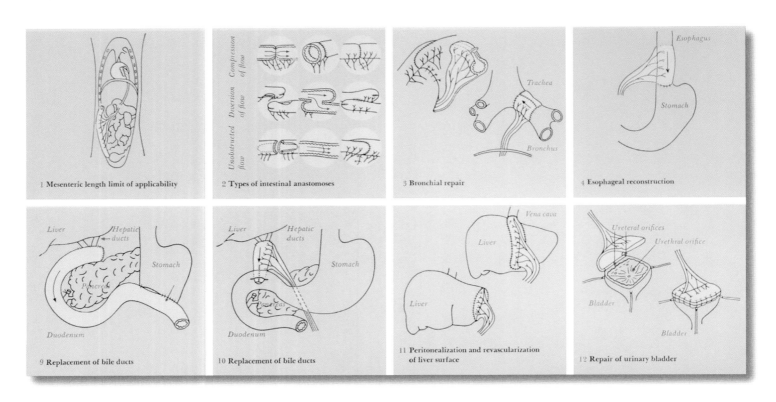

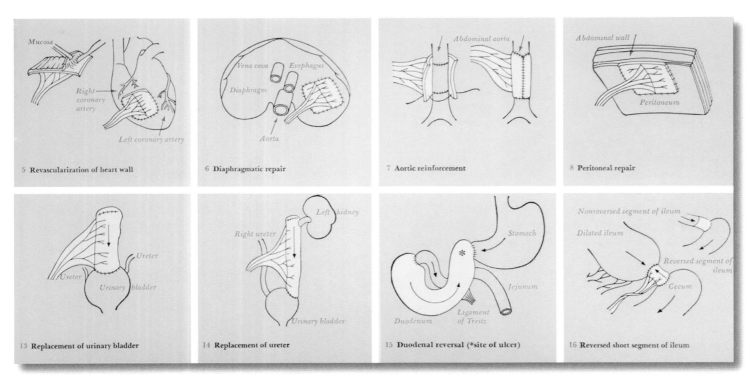

Image 3.2
Principle 2
Well-defined hierarchies.
Diagram from *SCOPE* magazine showing regulation
of blood glucose by pancreatic hormones.

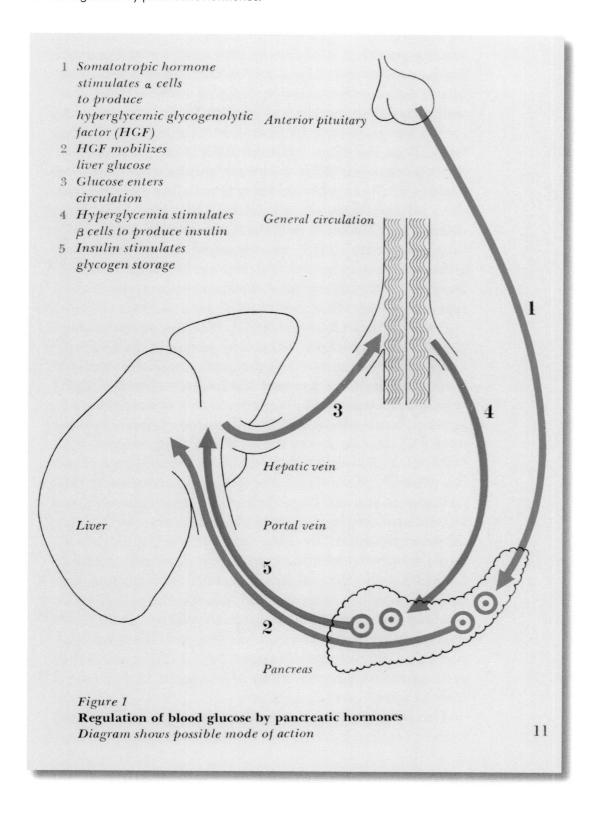

1 Somatotropic hormone
   stimulates α cells
   to produce
   hyperglycemic glycogenolytic
   factor (HGF)
2 HGF mobilizes
   liver glucose
3 Glucose enters
   circulation
4 Hyperglycemia stimulates
   β cells to produce insulin
5 Insulin stimulates
   glycogen storage

Anterior pituitary

General circulation

Hepatic vein

Liver

Portal vein

Pancreas

Figure 1
Regulation of blood glucose by pancreatic hormones
Diagram shows possible mode of action

11

Image 3.3
Principle 3
Logical visual structure of the information.
Diagram from *SCOPE* magazine showing the positive effect of a new
antibiotic, Mycifradin, in the intestine against bacteria after 3.5 hours.

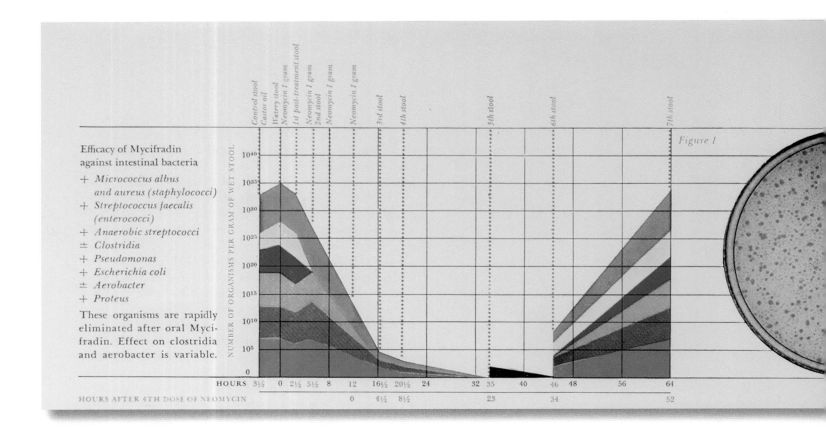

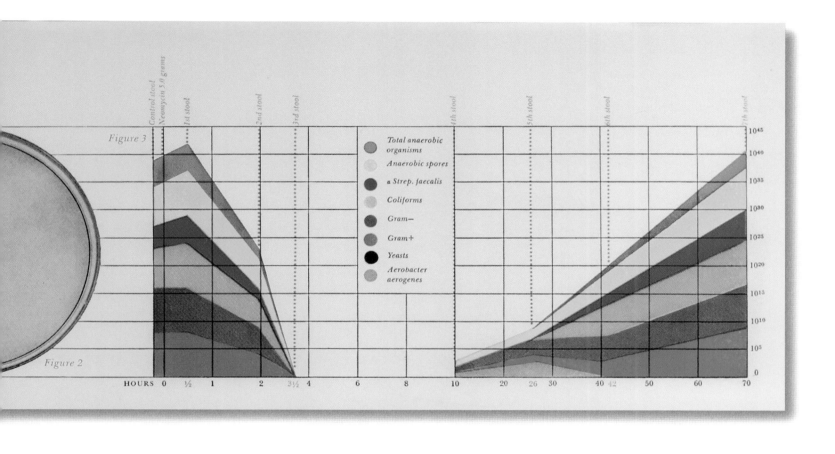

Figure 3

Figure 2

Total anaerobic organisms
Anaerobic spores
α Strep. faecalis
Coliforms
Gram−
Gram+
Yeasts
Aerobacter aerogenes

HOURS 0 ½ 1 2 3½ 4 6 8 10 20 26 30 40 42 50 60 70

Control stool
Neomycin 5.0 grams
1st stool
2nd stool
3rd stool
4th stool
5th stool
6th stool
7th stool

10^{45}
10^{40}
10^{35}
10^{30}
10^{25}
10^{20}
10^{15}
10^{10}
10^{5}
0

Image 3.4
Principle 4
Appropriate use of visual and textual language.
Spread from *SCOPE* magazine comparing tools of vision:
the eye and the microscope.

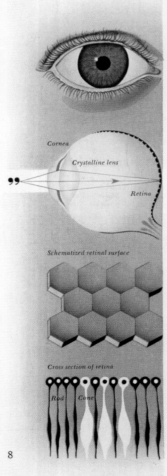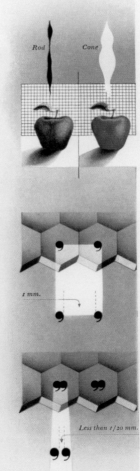

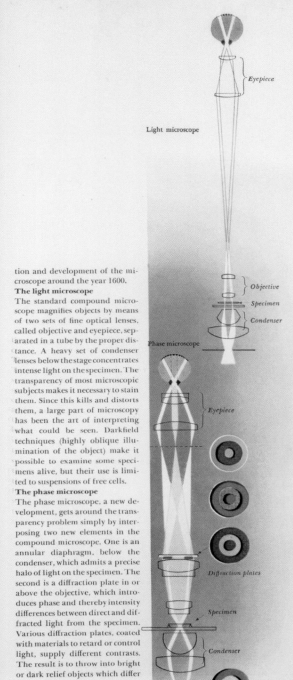

Light microscope

Phase microscope

tion and development of the microscope around the year 1600.

The light microscope

The standard compound microscope magnifies objects by means of two sets of fine optical lenses, called objective and eyepiece, separated in a tube by the proper distance. A heavy set of condenser lenses below the stage concentrates intense light on the specimen. The transparency of most microscopic subjects makes it necessary to stain them. Since this kills and distorts them, a large part of microscopy has been the art of interpreting what could be seen. Darkfield techniques (highly oblique illumination of the object) make it possible to examine some specimens alive, but their use is limited to suspensions of free cells.

The phase microscope

The phase microscope, a new development, gets around the transparency problem simply by interposing two new elements in the compound microscope. One is an annular diaphragm, below the condenser, which admits a precise halo of light on the specimen. The second is a diffraction plate in or above the objective, which introduces phase and thereby intensity differences between direct and diffracted light from the specimen. Various diffraction plates, coated with materials to retard or control light, supply different contrasts. The result is to throw into bright or dark relief objects which differ only slightly in refractive index

and hitherto had to be stained to be seen at all.

Limits of light

But any light microscope has its limits, set by the wavelength of visible light. This is measured in Angstrom units (one hundred-millionth of a centimeter) and ranges from 4,000 to 6,000 Ang. The light microscope's resolving power is limited to one-third the wavelength of white light, about 2,000 Ang. No object smaller than .0002 mm. can reflect or be distinguished by light. Some further resolution is secured by using quartz lenses and ultraviolet light (less than 3,000 Ang.); a new reflecting microscope is advancing this technique but it is cumbersome.

The electron microscope

The electron microscope, employing, instead of light, an electron beam with wavelength of only $\frac{1}{20}$ Ang., brought a great advance about fifteen years ago. It is almost a parallel of the light microscope, but uses magnetic instead of optical lenses. A beam of electrons from a hot cathode is focused by a magnetic condenser on the specimen, then focused for magnification through the objective, and finally thrown by the projector (instead of eyepiece) on a fluorescent screen or photographic plate. The electron microscope has over one hundred times more resolving power than the light microscope, and magnifications of over 10,000 as against 1,000.

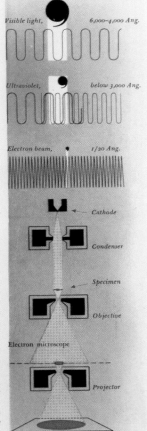

Electron microscope

13

Image 3.5
Principle 5
Purposeful use of visual variables.
Diagram from *SCOPE* magazine showing the type of medication (systemic, topical, both) preferred for lesions of various structures of the eye.

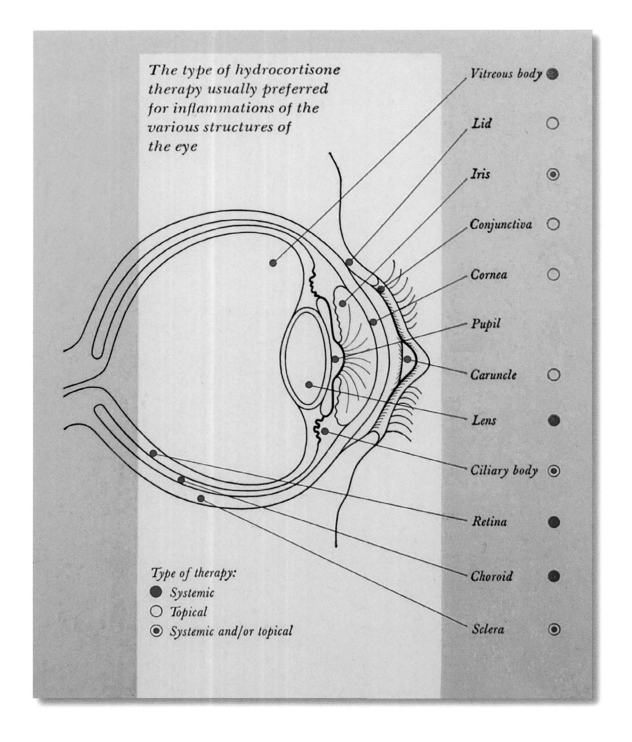

The type of hydrocortisone therapy usually preferred for inflammations of the various structures of the eye

Vitreous body
Lid
Iris
Conjunctiva
Cornea
Pupil
Caruncle
Lens
Ciliary body
Retina
Choroid
Sclera

Type of therapy:
● Systemic
○ Topical
◉ Systemic and/or topical

In order to achieve effective solutions, information design principles and research need to be followed by a designer with a curious and active mind, and a willingness to ask critical questions, investigate and learn. However, as Sutnar asserted, the solely mechanical application of graphic design principles will not produce high quality designs. To apply the principles effectively, designers should understand their values and meanings.[30] Burtin's design process, examined through Process Boxes presented in Chapters 4 to 8, demonstrates these qualities and the required understanding of the principles. To him, "form [was] not necessarily an added factor in this process, but a result of all previous considerations."[31] Burtin combined patient research and brilliant inventiveness to distill complex content into comprehensive, functional, simple and organized solutions. His legacy brings design closer to science, and adds value and credibility to information design.

3.3

Information Design's Need for Scientific Thinking

In 1967, Burtin stressed the need for visual communication to move beyond a designer expressing his or her personal style, to being concerned on a larger scale with the problem at hand. This in turn may have opened the door to making information design more common in other industries. Since Burtin's professional design years, many changes have occurred. Information design skills are valued across most industries, and professionals with these skills are in high demand to tackle the complexity of current challenges.[32] Institutions and organizations in various disciplines convey information in visual form for different purposes: to aid teaching and learning, to support the communication of ideas and unseen processes or thoughts, to improve the use of data, etc. Burtin would see this current phenomenon of design that connects commercial, technical, scientific and social requirements as making "the designer an essential partner in basic business planning rather than [someone simply] providing aesthetic pleasantry incidental to business."[33] Furthermore, information design has increasingly played a key role in facilitating better understanding across disciplines such as marketing, healthcare, finance, science, wayfinding and education.

Some of Burtin's ideas regarding the consolidation of "the new discipline in design"–Integration–remain unaddressed.[34] In other words, some key dimensions of the information design process are still not receiving the attention they deserve from the design community. Although Burtin felt that the visualization of scientific content was not an opportunity for self-expression, many information designers do follow an artistic approach to problem solving[35]: drawing and sketching are the core actions, and rigor and accuracy are relegated to second place or completely forgotten. Even when finished, information design work shows precision and engaging graphics, but the work may not be effective if the process that was followed wasn't systematic or rigorous, the design wasn't well thought through, and decisions weren't informed by research evidence. Not following the process that was suggested by Burtin results, more often than not, in solutions of poor quality or ineffective communication.

So, despite the current increase in the use of visual forms, effective communication and understanding are not always achieved. When design actions are performed without a rationale, and good decisions are made by accident, the resulting visualization of complex subjects can seem impenetrable to both the non-scientist and the expert.[36] In the contemporary scene, this frequently occurs because "there is too much emphasis on the production of design outputs and too little attention paid to the fundamental understanding of problems and people."[37]

Twenty years ago, British design researcher Nigel Cross said that the increasing complexity of design problems demanded the adoption of new or different problem-solving approaches.[38] Burtin's approach to visualizing scientific information, developed more than 60 years ago, could today provide the missing level of rigor and add the necessary scientific layer to the processes of contemporary design practitioners.

Table 3.2
Artistic and scientific approaches to design practice.

Artistic Approach		Scientific Approach	
1	Strong emphasis on prototype design	1	Strong emphasis on conceptual design: make sense of complexity; define ambiguous problems
2	Experience-informed decisions: secondary research for inspiration	2	Systematic way of working: follow specific steps to complete tasks before generating ideas
3	Strong focus on use of specialized digital tools	3	Research-informed decisions: secondary and ethnographic research to understand people first, then test solutions
4	Digital or manual drawing: sketch ideas, working and reworking until they are crystalline	4	Systems thinking: seek holistic understanding of the problem, context and influencing parties
5	Siloed way of working	5	Collaborative way of working: designers, content experts, audience, key stakeholders
6	Design of aesthetic outputs	6	Design of outputs integrating form and function

3.4
Burtin's Scientific Approach to Visual Communication

In the 1940s and '50s, many designers were commercial artists and illustrators without formal design education or training; as a result, they used an artistic approach, rooted in subjective personal taste and experience. The nature of Burtin's work called for a different approach to problem solving. The speed of information and technological advances in the 1950s generated a great amount of easily accessible and available content, but at the same time, made it difficult for the general population to catch up with all that was being produced. To help people make sense of the rapid changes they faced, Burtin adopted a scientific approach to design and the visualization of information, which has been found valuable by many others.[39]

Burtin's approach involved *rigor*, *integration* and *simplification*, since "selected aspects are all that can be shown of a far more complex reality."[40] When those selected aspects or essential elements have been appropriately chosen, they can be "understood more quickly and remembered more easily than reality itself" if the design is well-conceived. Burtin's systematic approach, informed by his love for science and the scientific method,[41] was not literally the scientific method itself, in that he did not start each project looking to rectify or reject a hypothesis.

Rather, he combined careful observation, systematic thinking and objective evidence with innovative ideas and a creative use of materials to develop ambitious, people-centered designs. We refer to Burtin's way of working as a scientific approach to visual communication.

Information designers benefit from working with a mixed-design approach like Burtin's because it puts a strong emphasis on conceptual design while combining systematic with unsystematic and creative actions.[42] John Chris Jones explains that first breaking down a design problem, and then systematizing conceptual design activities–not prototype design activities–is the key to this approach. Research and design principles were at the heart of Burtin's approach because they provided direction in making conceptual design more tangible and they supported decisions made throughout the process. This same approach might help bridge the existing gap between new information and understanding today because of the rapid development of scientific research and technology.[43] Adopting Burtin's scientific approach to visual communication is one way to improve the quality of information design work.

Diagrams illustrating Will Burtin's concept of Integration

Image 3.6
Diagram from *A-D Galley* brochure for *Integration: The New Discipline in Design* exhibition, showing component parts (typography, photography, artwork and color) of a magazine to indicate their distribution per page, 1948.

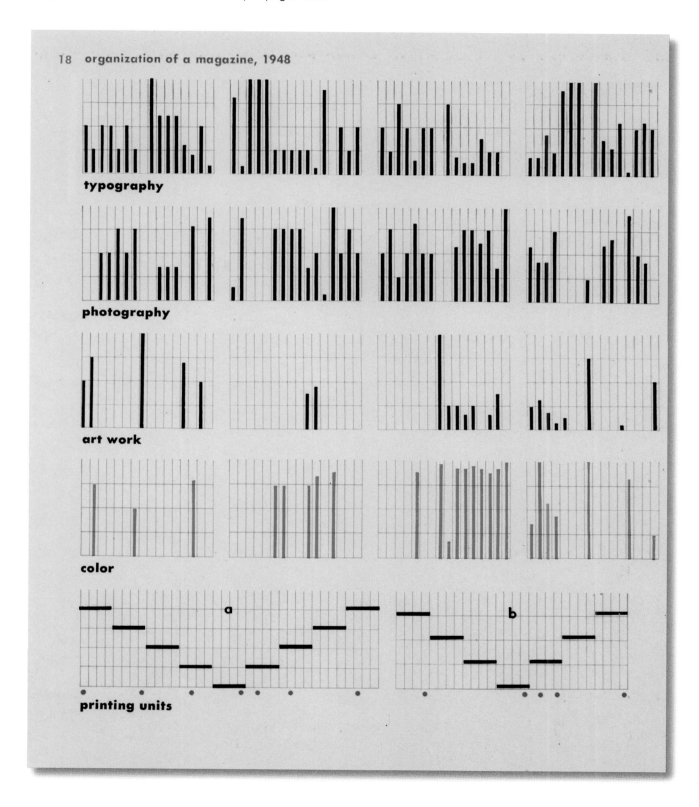

Image 3.7
Diagram from *Integration* brochure, showing the component parts
(color, drawings, photography and typography) of 64 pages of a
magazine to illustrate the harmonic integration of graphic elements
needed to visually communicate scientific knowledge with clarity,
while avoiding monotony, 1949.

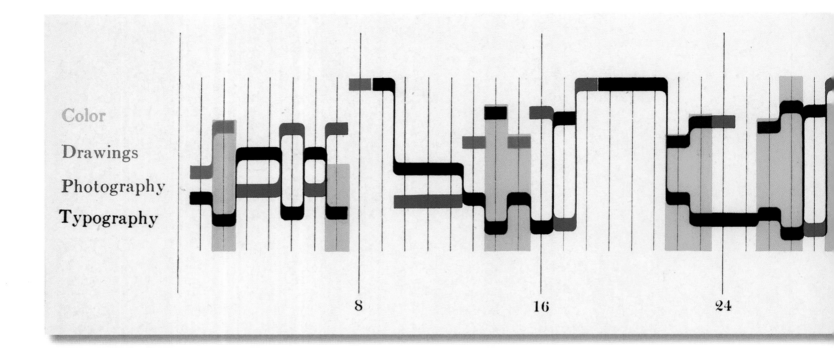

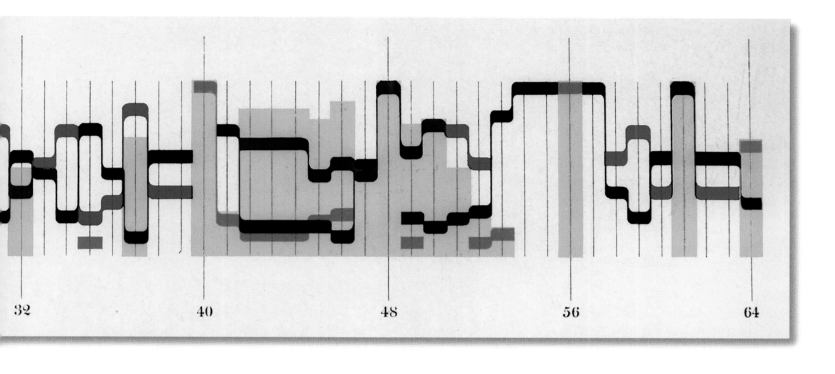

32   40   48   56   64

Diagram 3.1
Dimensions of information design including
Will Burtin's projects relevant to each.

3.5
Proposed Analytical Framework:
Dimensions of Information Design

In 1947, Burtin stressed that "[designers] are hardly concerned with the real thing, but the tool itself."[44] Similarly, contemporary information designers work with the latest technology and tools, but too often forget about the actual problem that needs to be solved.[45]

In the following chapters, we examine seven current dimensions of information design practice that constitute ongoing themes of discussion within and outside the design community:

1 **Purpose:** What is the aim of information design?
2 **Problem:** What constitutes an information design problem?
3 **Audience:** What is the role of the audience in the process?
4 **Approach:** What approach best supports information design work?
5 **Outcome:** What constitutes effective information design?
6 **Practice:** What is the value of information design?
7 **Education:** What is the role of information design in a learning process, and what knowledge and skills are needed to become an information designer?

Each dimension is discussed through the analysis of one or more of Burtin's projects and his written ideas, using his scientific approach as a framework. Thus, Burtin's projects are not presented chronologically. Instead, they are examined to illustrate and shed light on the seven dimensions listed above. Each project in this book illustrates one or more of Burtin's essential contributions to information design.

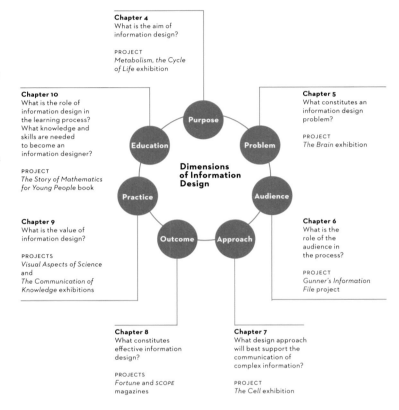

Chapter 4
What is the aim of information design?

PROJECT
Metabolism, the Cycle of Life exhibition

Chapter 10
What is the role of information design in the learning process? What knowledge and skills are needed to become an information designer?

PROJECT
The Story of Mathematics for Young People book

Chapter 5
What constitutes an information design problem?

PROJECT
The Brain exhibition

Chapter 9
What is the value of information design?

PROJECTS
Visual Aspects of Science and *The Communication of Knowledge* exhibitions

Chapter 6
What is the role of the audience in the process?

PROJECT
Gunner's Information File project

Chapter 8
What constitutes effective information design?

PROJECTS
Fortune and *SCOPE* magazines

Chapter 7
What design approach will best support the communication of complex information?

PROJECT
The Cell exhibition

Dimensions of Information Design — Purpose, Problem, Audience, Approach, Outcome, Practice, Education

Table 3.3
Will Burtin's major design projects. Projects showcased in this book are highlighted in bold.

Project Title	Type
Germany: 1920–1930s	
Fanal Flame brochure	Graphic and Editorial Design
Einst/Jetzt brochure	Graphic and Editorial Design
Sie Wollen Bauen brochure	Graphic and Editorial Design
***Kristall-Spiegelglas* brochure [Chapter 2]**	Graphic and Editorial Design
A Man Like You promotional piece	Graphic and Editorial Design
Fur Gas und Wasser brochure	Graphic and Editorial Design
Glas im Bau brochure	Graphic and Editorial Design
United States: 1930s	
Federal Works Agency exhibition at New York World's Fair	Exhibition Design
The Architectural Forum covers	Graphic Design
1940s	
First issue of *SCOPE* magazine	Information and Editorial Design
A/D journal cover and article	Information and Editorial Design
Gunner's *Information File* project: *Position Firing* manual; *Gunnery in the B-29* manual; *Gunnery in the A-26* manual; *This is Your Gun* manual [Chapter 6]	Information Design
***Fortune* magazine [Chapter 8]**	Art Direction
Graphis magazine	Information Design
Integration exhibition	Exhibition Design, Information Design
***SCOPE* magazine [Chapter 8]**	Art Direction, Information Design
1950s	
***The Cell* exhibition: model, brochure [Chapter 7]**	Exhibition Design, Information Design
Kalamazoo exhibition	Exhibition Design, Information Design
1960s	
***The Brain* exhibition: model, brochure [Chapter 9]**	Exhibition Design, Information Design, Editorial Design
Union Carbide's *Atomic Energy in Action* exhibition	Exhibition Design, Information Design
***Visual Aspects of Science* exhibition: model, brochure [Chapter 9]**	Exhibition Design, Information Design, Editorial Design
Comment 200 publication	Editorial Design
***Metabolism, the Cycle of Life* exhibition: model, brochure [Chapter 4]**	Exhibition Design, Information Design, Editorial Design
***Story of Mathematics for Young People* book [Chapter 10]**	Editorial Design, Information Design
Genes in Action exhibition: model, brochure	Exhibition Design, Information Design, Editorial Design
McGraw Hill exhibition	Exhibition Design, Information Design
Inflammation: Defense of Life exhibition	Exhibition Design, Information Design
The Many Worlds of Brunswick exhibition	Exhibition Design, Information Design
IBM Globe exhibition proposal	Exhibition Design, Information Design
1970s	
***The Communication of Knowledge* exhibition [Chapter 9]**	Exhibition Design, Information Design

NOTES

1   Will Burtin, "Integration, The New Discipline in Design:
    An Exhibition by Will Burtin from Nov. 9, 1948
    to January 14, 1949," *Graphis* 27 (1949): 235.

2   Richard Saul Wurman, *Information Anxiety*
    (New York: Doubleday, 1989); Wurman,
    Information Anxiety 2, rev. ed. (Indianapolis: Que, 2001).

3   Edward R. Tufte, *The Visual Display of
    Quantitative Information* (Cheshire, CT: Graphics Press, 1983);
    Tufte, *Visual Explanations: Images and Quantities,
    Evidence and Narrative* (Cheshire, CT: Graphics Press, 1997).

4   Rune Pettersson, "Information Design–Principles
    and Guidelines," *Journal of Visual Literacy* 29, no. 2
    (September 2010): 167–182.

5   Jorge Frascara, *Information Design as Principled Action:
    Making Information Accessible, Relevant, Understandable,
    and Usable* (Champaign, IL: Common Ground, 2015).

6   Inge Gobert and Johan van Looveren,
    Thoughts on Designing Information
    (Zurich: Lars Müller, 2014).

7   Sheila Pontis, *Making Sense of Field Research:
    A Practical Guide for Information Designers*
    (Oxfordshire, UK: Routledge, 2018).

8   Rob Waller, "Information Design: How the Disciplines
    Work Together" (conference paper, Vision Plus 1, Götzis,
    Austria, August 1995), reprinted as "Technical Paper 14"
    (Reading, UK: Simplification Centre,
    University of Reading, 2011),
    https://www.robwaller.org/SC14DisciplinesTogether.
    pdf; Sheila Pontis and Michael Babwahsingh, "Communicating
    Complexity and Simplicity: Rediscovering the Fundamentals
    of Information Design" (conference paper, 2CO–
    Communicating Complexity, Sardinia, Italy,
    October 2013), 244–61; "Information Design:
    Core Competencies–What Information Designers Know
    and Can Do," Information Design Exchange (idx),
    Austria, IIID Public Library, August 31, 2007,
    https:// www.iiid.net/PublicLibrary/idx-Core-Competencies-
    What-information-designers-know-and-can-do.pdf.

9   Harry Robin, *The Scientific Image: From Cave to Computer*
    (New York: W.H. Freeman, 1993).

10 Ibid.

11 Tufte, *Visual Explanations*, 27–37; Tufte, *Visual Display*, 24.

12 Tufte, *Beautiful Evidence*
    (Cheshire, CT: Graphics Press, 2006), 122–139.

13 Howard Wainer, *Visual Revelations: Graphical Tales of Fate
    and Deception from Napoleon Bonaparte to Ross Perot*
    (New York: Copernicus, 1997).

14 Ladislav Sutnar, *Visual Design in Action*, ed. Reto Caduff and
    Steven Heller, 1st ed. (New York: Hastings House, 1961);
    facsimile reprint (Zurich: Lars Müller, 2015).

15 Frank H. Netter, *The CIBA Collection of Medical Illustrations*
    vol. 1, *Nervous System*, 11th ed. (West Caldwell, NJ: CIBA, 1975).

16 Philip B. Meggs, *A History of Graphic Design*, 3rd ed.
    (New York: John Wiley, 1998).

17 Burtin and Lawrence P. Lessing, "Interrelations,"
    Graphis 22, vol. 4 (1948): 108.

18 Ibid.

19 Burtin, "Thoughts on Three-Dimensional Science
    Communications," *Dot Zero*, no. 4 (Summer 1967: World's Fairs).

20 James Foley and William Ribarsky, "Next-Generation
    Data Visualization Tools," in *Scientific Visualization*,
    by Lawrence J. Rosenblum et al.
    (London: Academic Press, 1994): 103–127,
    https://smartech.gatech.edu/bitstream/handle/1853/3594/94-27.
    pdf?sequence=1&isAllowed=y.

21 G. Scott Owen, "Definitions and Rationale for Visualization,"
    Siggraph, 1996, 1, https://www.cs.rit.edu/usr/local/pub/ncs/
    hypervis/visgoals/visgoal2.htm.

22 Colin Ware, *Information Visualization: Perception for Design*
    (Netherlands: Elsevier, 2012), 2.

23 Ibid.; James Gleick, *The Information: A History, a Theory,
    a Flood* (New York: Pantheon, 2012).

24 Robin, *Scientific Image*, 9.

25 Pontis, "Guidelines for Conceptual Design to
    Assist Diagram Creators in Information Design Practice"
    (Ph.D. dissertation, University of the Arts London, 2012).

26 Stephen M. Kosslyn, *Graph Design for the Eye and Mind*
    (New York: Oxford University Press, 2006), 5.

27 Pontis and Babwahsingh, "Communicating," 244–61.

28 Pontis, *Making Sense*.

29 Burtin and Lessing, "Interrelations," 108.

30 Sutnar, *Visual Design*.

31 Burtin, "Untitled Notes" (unpublished, n.d.): 1,
    Will Burtin Papers, 64, Cary Graphic Design Archive, RIT

32 Pettersson, "Information Design"; Frascara,
    Information Design.

33 Burtin, "2-D or 3-D?" (unpublished manuscript, 1964: 1),
    Will Burtin Papers, 92.5, Cary Graphic Design Archive, RIT.

34 Burtin, "Integration," *Graphis*.

35 Steven Heller and Rick Landers,
    Infographic Designers' Sketchbooks
    (New York: Princeton Architectural Press, 2014).

36 Burtin, *Integration–The New Discipline in Design*,
    exhibition brochure (Chicago: Art Directors Club, 1949),
    Will Burtin Papers, 55.6 and 90.12–90.13,
    Cary Graphic Design Archive, RIT.

37 Pontis, *Making Sense*, xv.

38 Nigel Cross, "Designerly Ways of Knowing: Design Discipline
    versus Design Science," *Design Issues* 17, no. 3 (2001): 49–55,
    http://oro.open.ac.uk/3281/1/Designerly-_DisciplinevScience.pdf.

39 Patrick Burgoyne, "Will Burtin: Forgotten Master of Design,"
    Creative Review, November 27, 2007, https://www.
    creativereview.co.uk/will-burtin-forgotten-master-of-design/;
    Lorraine Wild, "Will Burtin: Design and Science,"
    Design Observer (April 15, 2009), http://designobserver.com/
    feature/will-burtin-design-and-science/8337/;
    Heller, "Will Burtin's Beauty," *Print* (May 31, 2013); Steven Brower,
    "Design History 101: From Pharma to Fortune, Designer
    Will Burtin Has Range,"*AIGA: Eye on Design*, November 12, 2015,
    https://eyeondesign.aiga.org/from-pharma-to-fortune-
    designer-will-burtin-has-range/.

40 Burtin, "Thoughts on Three-Dimensional," 1.

41 Ibid., 1.

42 John Chris Jones, *Design Methods*, 2nd ed.
    (New York: John Wiley, 1992); Pontis, "Guidelines."

43 Wurman, *Anxiety* (1989).

44 Burtin, "Theory of Design Course Lectures"
    (Lecture 1, February 20, 1947), 3, Will Burtin Papers, 96.7,
    Cary Graphic Design Archive, RIT.

45 Wurman, *Anxiety 2* (2001).

Image 4.1
Will Burtin with the *Metabolism, the Cycle of Life*
exhibition for the Upjohn Company, 1963.

CHAPTER 4

Purpose

4.1

Facilitating Understanding

For Burtin, "the real difference between 1920 and 1966 [was] that the problems of drastic simplification and clear exposition assumed a far more pressing relevance." Clear exposition was critical to Burtin because of "increased communication density, greatly extended range and [the] inescapable present."[1] In 2021, the complexity of our society's problems has grown exponentially and our need for clarity and understanding has become even more pressing. Complexity, a constantly evolving phenomenon, has always been manifested throughout history. But how individuals perceive and deal with it has changed from one time period to another.[2] This does not mean that, while complexity is an intrinsic part of life, "the confusion, ambiguity and lack of understanding that may result from [it]" are somehow *necessary*.[3] Instead, information designers can help make sense of complexity by bringing order to confusing and ambiguous situations.

Burtin maintained that designers can understand problems and gain exciting insights into them "through unceasing comparison and interrelation of factors" that then enable them to "depict even that which had been invisible."[4] Information designers can lead the way to understanding by "encouraging awareness of connections," which will then facilitate the identification of patterns.[5] When designers break down complexity, extract its essential elements, and communicate those elements through visual means, people can more rapidly digest and process complexity.[6]

As the previous chapter explained, this process of visualizing complexity involves both digesting and simplifying content according to meanings and then regrouping those meanings on different levels depending on a project's specifics.[7] Note the distinction between creating something simple and something simplistic. When a visualization is simplistic, Richard Saul Wurman writes, it "becomes vague and meaningless" because "there is nothing to relate to it."[8] Consultants Alan Siegel and Irene Etzkorn feel that the key to adopting simplicity in the world of business is understanding "what is essential and meaningful as opposed to what is not, then ruthlessly eliminating the latter, while putting emphasis and focus on the former."[9] Burtin would have agreed with them.

"The visual quality of a designed model can distort meaning sometimes," Burtin wrote, "putting [the] primary emphasis on appearance factors rather than on those ideas which are the reason for its being."[10] In other words, as Wurman has asserted, "Understanding is not about simplification and minimalization; it's about organization and clarification."[11]

Burtin's approach to visualization was grounded in his lifelong career focus on combining "convenience, clarity, usability, timeliness, [and] beauty"–words also used by Siegel and Etzkorn to describe how to conquer complexity.[12]

One of Burtin's methods of communicating complexity–of making the invisible visible and comprehensible–was by creating models, both three-dimensional and otherwise. He reflected:

> It seems necessary to remember that 'models' of thoughts, structures, or processes need not always be visual in a representational-image sense. There are verbal models, or graphs, or typography, or colors that may be suitable vehicles to explain ideas with a maximum of efficiency and a minimum of means. One must also keep the difference between explanation and the real event, or fact, constantly in mind. The first is a symbolic and tentative interpretation by which we establish contact between human ideas, or knowledge, and people. The second is at times elusive and its meaning may not always be translatable without distortion.[13]

Burtin's use of models expanded to include physical, three-dimensional creations that became his most remarkable mode of design. He believed that, in order to convey meaning appropriately, three-dimensional medical communication models must have three essential features:

> *First*: The model must enhance a feeling for–and not distort understanding of–the reality behind the communication by limiting its contents to clearly apparent objectives.

> *Second*: The design analysis of the model must be motivated by a devotion to clarity, to assure that its three-dimensional form is the most economical, time-saving and meaningful way to convey the information.

> *Third*: Organization and translation of data into space, scale, material, form, color, motion, sound or timed sequence must result in such a simple and yet intense sensory and logical structured experience that the model is easy to remember.[14]

Image 4.2
Will Burtin with the *Metabolism, the Cycle of Life* exhibition, 1963.

All of Burtin's three-dimensional models were conceived and built with these three features in mind, in order to make the subject understandable and comprehensible to its intended audience. Siegel and Etzkorn would have described Burtin's projects as achieving "transparency (laying bare the underlying truth, whatever it reveals), clarity (expressing meaning clearly and simply), and usability (making something fit for its purpose)."[15] Burtin's work, whether simple or complex, in large-scale exhibitions or small-scale representations (magazines), translated particular aspects of the complex invisible world into a clear, visible reality that could be understood and, most importantly, remembered.

In short, the core goal of information design is to facilitate understanding in order to help people achieve their own goals, such as making sense of scientific concepts, getting from point A to point B, understanding how to assemble a piece of new furniture or using a new device. The next section shows how one of Burtin's exhibitions helped the general public and expert audiences achieve their own goals: better understanding a scientific process.

4.2
Metabolism, the Cycle of Life Exhibition

The metabolic process is essential to life, but its complexity can make it hard to understand. In order to clearly explain this process, Burtin created an experiential exhibition where he greatly enlarged the physical scale of the process to show key metabolic chemical reactions, and used familiar analogies to communicate its core characteristics.

In the 1950s, "the volume of literature on metabolism, and the rate at which new information accumulated, were so formidable that a Presidential Commission was formed to study means of condensing information, so that further progress should not be hindered by communication difficulties."[16] To make this topic more accessible to both expert audiences and the general public, Burtin designed the *Metabolism, the Cycle of Life* exhibition in 1963 for The Upjohn Company, a pharmaceutical manufacturer in Kalamazoo, Michigan. The *Metabolism* exhibition was centered on the mitochondrion itself, showing its basic structure and demonstrating core functions through a large-scale model. To accomplish this, Burtin first worked with prestigious medical consultants, including Nobel Laureate Albert Szent-Gyorgyi and Rockefeller University scientist Keith Porter. These conversations helped him to familiarize with the chemical reactions and processes that occur in the body to maintain life.

Burtin learned that mitochondria serve as the body's main energy source, generating energy by breaking up the chemical bonds of glucose in the cell. Mitochondria also store and support the enzyme systems that regulate and transform (metabolize) the body's organic chemistry. To represent these processes, Burtin based the exhibition "entirely on moving lights, colors, and shape symbols." He explained that "the order by which the mitochondrion– the 'powerhouse' of the cell–provides energy that alters and builds up molecules into complex enzymes and hormones that produce energy for life-maintaining functions, is demonstrated as one coherent process that takes on several forms."[17]

Top
Image 4.3
Metabolism, the Cycle of Life exhibition,
small-scale model, 1963.

Bottom
Image 4.4
Metabolism, the Cycle of Life exhibition,
real size, 1963.

The structure of the exhibition was a circular platform containing a continuous eight-ring spiral structure with moving light bands expanding from the center, into which the observer could walk to watch performances in eight spheres, one fastened to each ring. "Each of these spheres showed metabolic events and the end product of each event was the 'starter' product of the next."[18] The spiral rings converged in the center of the circular platform, where a structure of a mitochondrion was placed. Lights moved from the inside of the rings to the center, from which they emerged again with much stronger intensity to create a sphere. "Here they set off the light and color sequence of a metabolic event. Upon its completion, the lights emerged again at the bottom of the sphere to return via the spiral ring to the center, to move from there into the next sphere. Thus, the motion of light guided the observer from one sphere to the next, as he walked around on the circular platform."[19]

The spiral and lights indicated that the metabolic process is a cycle that never stops. Burtin's eight half-spheres attached to the pipes demonstrated the principle that "energy *production* plus energy *use* equals *new* energy for energy *production*" for the eight key uses of energy. [20] In Burtin's words, the center "raised circular platform, accessible from all sides and seemingly suspended inside the spiral" connected "all eight demonstrations that deal with the utilization and production" of energy, like "fat, sugar, heat, etc."[21]

Burtin explained how he designed the exhibition as something to be experienced:

> At reading height in eight half-spheres, important specific chemical transitions are demonstrated through moving light and color sequences which start at the moment the lights from the spiral enter into the top half-spheres. When the motion inside the half-spheres is completed, light in the spiral pipe commences from below the half-sphere and returns into the mitochondrion, there to be charged again for the next metabolic sequence in the next half-sphere.[22]

This description reveals Burtin's thorough understanding of the topic he was working with and his ability to identify and communicate key details with clarity in the model. To experience the exhibition and understand the metabolic process, visitors just needed to pay attention (visually) and follow (physically) the movement of the lights.

To complement the exhibition, Burtin designed a detailed take-away brochure titled *Metabolism: the Process of Life.*"[23] The brochure demanded the same technical accuracy as the exhibition, but its content was directed at doctors and scientists rather than the lay public. It combined a scientific explanation of the metabolic process with full-page diagrams representing key and hard-to-understand concepts, like the structure of the mitochondrion, and how the process functions. (see images 4.5 to 4.11.)

Using a square format (8.5 × 8.5 in.), Burtin created diagrams to visually explain main chemical reactions taking place in the mitochondrion. For example, page 4 showed a visual representation of the process involved in the active transport of glucose; (see image 4.7) pages 6 and 8 illustrated the processes of the synthesis of glycogen and fat, respectively; (see images 4.8 and 4.9) and page 18 visualized heat generation. (see image 4.10.) These diagrams were created on top of a photographic image of a mitochondrion, and key components of the process were graphically coded using various shapes and colors, as indicated on a key placed on the left side of the page. The flow and steps of the processes were indicated with arrows. Additional photographic material was also displayed in the brochure.

Image 4.5
Cover, *Metabolism: the Process of Life* brochure, 1963.

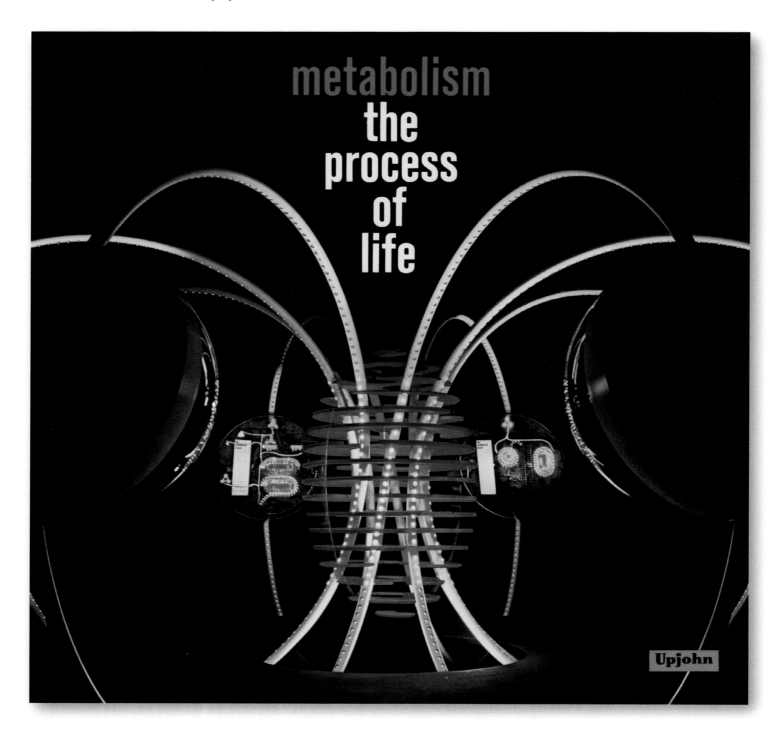

Images 4.6 and 4.7
Inside pages, *Metabolism: the Process of Life* brochure, 1963.

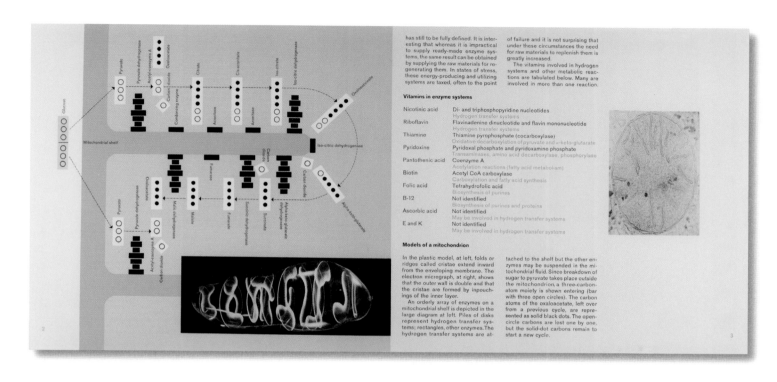

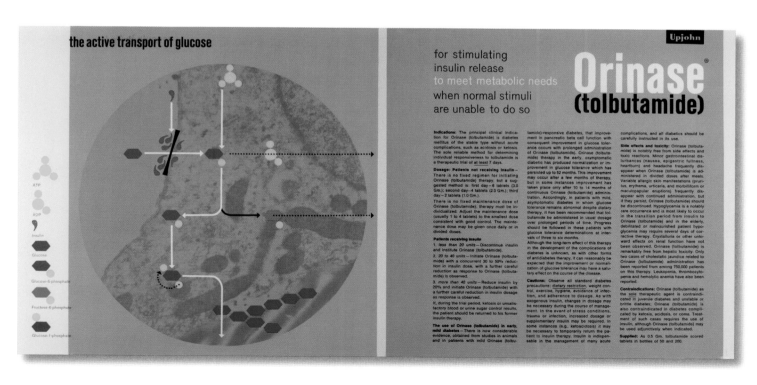

Images 4.8 and 4.9
Inside pages, *Metabolism* brochure.

the synthesis of glycogen

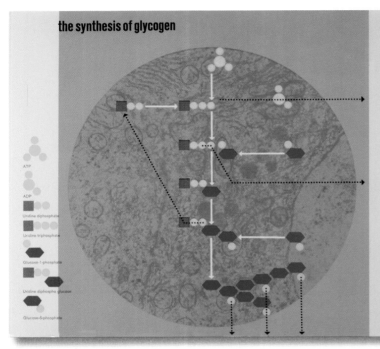

ATP

ADP

Uridine diphosphate

Uridine triphosphate

Glucose-1-phosphate

Uridine diphospho glucose

Glucose-6-phosphate

After entering the cell, some of the glucose is usually broken down to form energy. Any that is not needed for this purpose, however, is either converted to glycogen or to fat for storage. Glycogen stores usually have first claim on such an excess so that the process of glycogen synthesis will be taken up first.

It was formerly thought that glycogen was formed by reversing the process of glycogen breakdown which occurs with phosphorylase—an enzyme which seems to require pyridoxal for its proper function. Long-chain carbohydrate molecules can be made in this way but it appears that this is not the usual method of synthesizing glycogen in animal tissue. A somewhat more complicated process involving uridine diphosphate-glucose, and some preformed glycogen as a sort of primer, is the preferred pathway.

Like so many biological processes this one is cyclical, so the starting point is somewhat arbitrary. The first step can, however, be considered to be the formation of uridine triphosphate from uridine diphosphate and ATP, adenosine triphosphate. This is the first reaction in the diagram. Glucose-1-phosphate then interacts with uridine triphosphate to form uridine diphosphoglucose with the release of two phosphate radicals. This reaction is catalyzed by uridine diphosphoglucose pyrophosphorylase. It is the second reaction in the diagram. Uridine diphosphoglucose is next shown as combining with glucose-6-phosphate to form a diose phosphate with the release of the uridine diphosphate which then returns to the pool for reuse. Ordinarily this does not happen; the glucose moiety of the uridine diphosphoglucose is attached to one of the branches of a pre-existing gly-

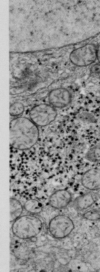

Glycogen granules appear as black dots in this electron micrograph of a rat liver.

cogen molecule thereby enlarging the molecule by one glucose unit. This latter reaction is accomplished through the instrumentality of uridine diphosphoglucose glycogen transglucosylase. This enzyme apparently requires glucose-6-phosphate to activate it. Also a branching enzyme amylo (1,4-1,6) transglucosidase is required to produce the highly branched structure characteristic of normal glycogen.

When glucose is first phosphorylated, it is glucose-6-phosphate that is formed. Before being converted to glycogen, however, glucose-6-phosphate must first be converted to glucose-1-phosphate. To accomplish this, glucose-1, 6-diphosphate is required. The reaction is a curious one, being a device to avoid an intramolecular shift of a phosphate radical. In the presence of a transphosphorylase a molecule of glucose-1, 6-diphosphate transfers the phosphate in its six position to the one position of the molecule of glucose-6-phosphate, thus being converted to a molecule of glucose-1-phosphate. Hence, a molecule of glucose-6-phosphate is converted to a molecule of glucose-1,6-diphosphate and finally to a molecule of glucose-1-phosphate.

In certain tissues such as muscle and probably liver, insulin increases the rate of glycogen formation. These effects are observed in intact tissue and their mechanism has not been defined by **in vitro** experiments. They may be direct or indirect, dependent on the acceleration of the transport mechanism. C. Villar-Palasi and J. Larner, for example, observed an insulin-induced increase in glycogen synthetase activity in rat diaphragm, but their experiments did not permit pinpointing of the insulin effect.

7

the synthesis of fat

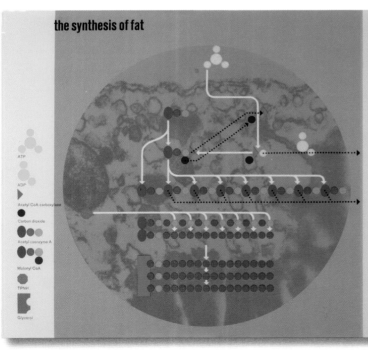

ATP

ADP

Acetyl CoA carboxylase

Carbon dioxide

Acetyl coenzyme A

Malonyl CoA

TPNH

Glycerol

The idea that fat is utilized for energy by oxidative attack on the β carbon atom has been known for a long time, the key role of the pantothenic acid-containing Co-enzyme A was a later development, and the localization of the process to the mitochondrion a recent discovery. With the discovery that the reactions of β oxidation were reversible, it was thought that fat synthesis occurred by reversing the process of breakdown. Indeed, subsequent investigation has demonstrated that fat is actually synthesized by this route. However, in recent years there have been numerous observations that indicated that there must also be another route of synthesis.

It is now clear from the work of S. J. Wakil and associates that there are two routes of fat synthesis, one the reversal of the classical β oxidation route in the mitochondria and another in the cytoplasm outside the mitochondria. It further appears that while the β oxidation pathway is the route of the breakdown of fat, the recently discovered extra-mitochondrial pathway is the more important route for synthesis. This pathway builds the greater part of the fat that is synthesized up to the stage of palmitate. The adding of additional carbon atoms to make longer chains is then carried out in the mitochondria by the classical process.

It is this new extra-mitochondrial pathway of fat synthesis that is represented in the diagram. The first stage of the reaction probably is the temporary union of the carbon dioxide to the biotin-containing enzyme (acetyl CoA carboxylase) with the utilization of ATP which is converted to ADP and inorganic phosphate in the process. This activated CO_2 is then united with acetyl Coenzyme

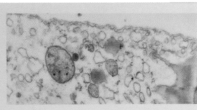

Fat cell of a rat showing active fat synthesis as indicated by thickened cell membrane and many vacuoles in the cytoplasm.

A to form malonyl CoA; manganese is also a co-factor in this reaction.

The malonyl CoA thus formed is then used to form palmityl CoA. This is accomplished by a special SH-containing enzyme purified and identified by Wakil and Ganguly. Acetyl CoA and TPNH are also required. It appears that two of the carbon atoms of the palmitic acid are furnished by one molecule of acetyl CoA and the rest by molecules of malonyl CoA, a molecule of CO_2 being released from each molecule of malonyl CoA in the process. The diagram consequently indicates first the carbon dioxide and then the Co-enzyme A running off at this stage. Next, TPNH is shown furnishing the hydrogen to reduce the oxidized groups and produce a typical saturated fatty acid. Finally, a union of three molecules of palmitic acid with glycerol to form neutral fat is indicated.

The exact order and nature of the complicated chemical transformations that must occur in the conversion of acetyl CoA and malonyl CoA

to palmityl CoA are not yet known but the end result is clear.

The difficulty that the diabetic patient has in synthesizing fat seems to be interference with the extra-mitochondrial system of fat synthesis. D. M. Gibson and D. D. Hubbard assayed livers of diabetic and starved animals for their content of the two key enzymes required in this process. They found that the activity of acetyl CoA carboxylase that converts acetyl CoA to malonyl CoA was normal, but that the activity of the enzyme that converts malonyl CoA to palmityl CoA was much reduced. Since both TPNH from the hexose monophosphate pathway and glycerol from glycolysis are needed for the formation of fat, their availability influences the rate of fat synthesis. Nevertheless, they do not seem to be the factors that limit fat formation in liver slices from diabetic animals because even if they are supplied in adequate amounts these preparations are still unable to synthesize fat normally. It would therefore seem that the most important limiting factor is the decreased activity of the enzyme that converts malonyl CoA to palmityl CoA just described.

9

Images 4.10 and 4.11
Inside pages, *Metabolism* brochure.

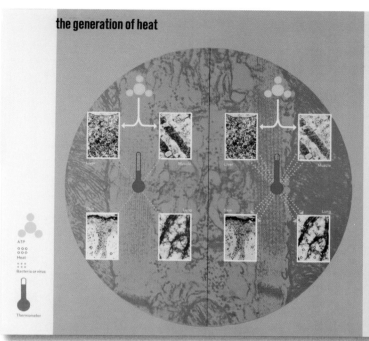

Heat has long been regarded as the common denominator of energy transformations. However, its production in most such transformations is often an indication of and a measure of inefficiency, e.g., the heat produced in transforming electricity into light is a waste product. This is true to a considerable extent in metabolic processes. The chemical energy expended to synthesize a needed product is not all used for this purpose; inevitably some appears as heat. Likewise, not all of the chemical energy expended for muscle contraction is converted to mechanical work; some again appears as heat.

Warm-bloodedness develops

How in the process of evolution the transition from cold-bloodedness to warm-bloodedness occurred is obscure. It may have been that the first warm-blooded animal was an unusually inefficient creature, but, if so, this defect has proved to be a great asset. It made possible a creature who produced enough heat so that his activity was largely independent of the temperature of his environment. Thus, with cooling environments on the earth the ponderous dinosaurs succumbed and the small but much more adaptable mammals and birds survived.

Consequently, although the maintenance of body temperature is one of the important functions of metabolism, and although a considerable part of the energy derived from food is used for this purpose, there is no specific set of chemical reactions whose function is solely the production of heat. Body heat is largely a product of numerous exothermal reactions that are performing other tasks as well.

Since the speeds of metabolic reactions are to varying extents regulated by the temperature, it is necessary that the body temperature be constant. This is accomplished in two ways: by regulating heat production and heat elimination.

Temperature regulation

Heat production, being dependent on body activity, varies considerably and is primarily regulated by factors other than the need for heat. However, where extra heat is needed, it can be generated by various means such as by shivering which causes increased muscular activity with consequent heat production. The most important regulatory mechanism, therefore, is that of heat loss.

Heat is lost largely either by radiation from the skin or from the lungs by way of the expired air. Regulation, therefore, is accomplished by control of the circulation to those surfaces. In addition, sweating can be stimulated and the rate of respiration increased where large amounts of heat must be dissipated. Fever results when either too much heat is produced or insufficient is dissipated or both.

The regulation of temperature is controlled by a center in the medulla and, of course, injury to this center can also give rise to abnormal body temperature. Space does not permit any discussion of the complex heat regulatory system, although a great deal of work has been done on the subject. Rather, we will trace briefly the much less well defined subject of heat production.

As indicated in the diagram, ATP is the source of much of the energy for heat production as it was for the various other important metabolic functions previously described. As indicated, muscle and liver are the tissues in which most of the body heat is produced. Unfortunately, all the reactions which contribute to heat production cannot be listed, but they are many. The liver, which is the great seat of chemical transformations, houses many of these reactions, and the heat liberated is disseminated by the rich circulation that passes through it. Muscle, of course, produces heat with every contraction and this, too, is carried away by the blood. The skin and lungs, the dissipators of heat, are also richly supplied with blood vessels which bring them the heat that must be radiated away.

A source of considerable heat appears to be the direct breakdown of ATP to ADP or the monophosphate, AMP, which apparently occurs if the compound remains long unused due to its inherent instability. Representation of this reaction, therefore, symbolizes in the diagram both the heat incidental to the reactions that derive their energy from this breakdown and the heat produced by the breakdown uncoupled with another reaction.

Fever

On the right of the diagram the situation in fever is indicated where bacterial toxins or other pyrogenic substances stimulate abnormal heat production. Sometimes the heat regulatory mechanisms are interfered with by these toxic substances and the heat is not efficiently transferred to the radiating surfaces, e.g., a vasoconstriction may be produced. However, more heat than normal may actually be radiated from the skin and lungs, but not enough to prevent a rise in temperature.

19

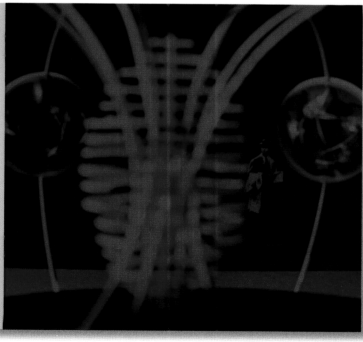

Image 4.6 Detail
Diagram from *Metabolism* brochure.

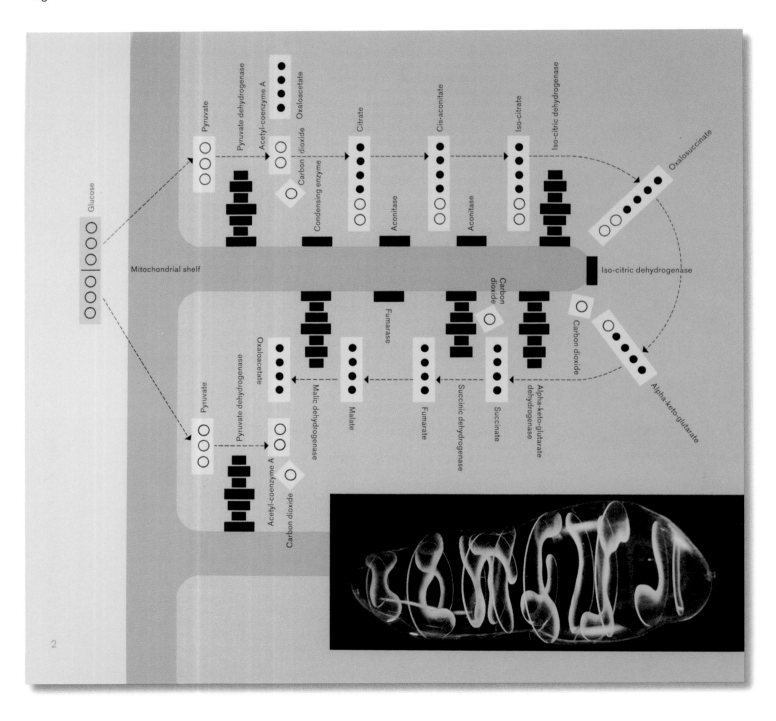

Image 4.9 Detail
Diagram from *Metabolism* brochure.

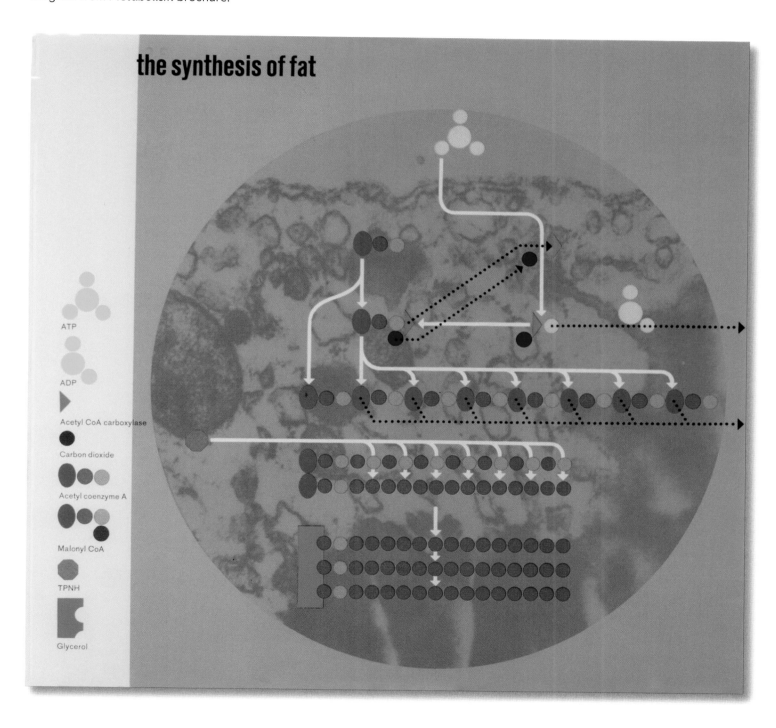

the synthesis of fat

ATP

ADP

Acetyl CoA carboxylase

Carbon dioxide

Acetyl coenzyme A

Malonyl CoA

TPNH

Glycerol

NOTES

1 Will Burtin, "Reflections on Graphic Design"
(unpublished manuscript, 1966), 4,
Will Burtin Papers, 93.5,
Cary Graphic Design Archive, RIT

2 Don Norman, *Living with Complexity*
(Cambridge, MA: MIT Press, 2011).

3 Sheila Pontis and Michael Babwahsingh,
"Communicating Complexity and Simplicity:
Rediscovering the Fundamentals of Information Design"
(conference paper, 2CO-Communicating Complexity,
Sardinia, Italy, October 2013), 246.

4 Burtin, *Integration-The New Discipline in Design*,
exhibition brochure (Chicago: Art Directors Club, 1949), 7,
Will Burtin Papers, 55.6 and 90.12-90.13,
Cary Graphic Design Archive, RIT.

5 Richard S. Wurman, "Hats," *Design Quarterly* 145 (1989): 1-32.

6 Pontis and Babwahsingh, "Communicating."

7 Alan Siegel and Irene Etzkorn,
Simple: Conquering the Crisis of Complexity
(New York: Twelve, 2013).

8 Wurman, "Hats," 5.

9 Siegel and Etzkorn, *Simple*, 7.

10 Burtin, "Reflections," 9.

11 Wurman, "Hats," 5.

12 Siegel and Etzkorn, *Simple*, 6.

13 Burtin, "Reflections," 17.

14 Burtin, "Thoughts on Three-Dimensional Science
Communications," *Dot Zero* 4 (Summer 1967: World's Fairs).

15 Siegel and Etzkorn, *Simple*, 7.

16 Burtin, "Reflections," 16.

17 Burtin, "A Program in Print: Upjohn and Design"
Print 10, no. 4 (insert, May/June 1955), 4;
also in Will Burtin Papers, 77.5,
Cary Graphic Design Archive, RIT.

18 Burtin, "Reflections," 16.

19 Ibid., 17.

20 Ibid., 18.

21 Ibid.

22 Ibid.

23 *Metabolism: The Process of Life* exhibition brochure
(Kalamazoo, MI: Upjohn, 1963). Will Burtin Papers, 74.4,
Cary Graphic Design Archive, RIT.

24 Burtin, "Reflections," 18.

25 R. Roger Remington and Robert S.P. Fripp,
Design and Science: The Life and Work of Will Burtin
(Hampshire, UK: Lund Humphries, 2007), 105.

4.3
Process Box 1
Case Study 1: *Metabolism, the Cycle of Life* **Exhibition (1963)**

Conceptual Design

Understanding and Framing the Problem
"This model had to solve three problems on a visual level:
1 To determine a method by which specific examples of metabolic processes could be organized and interrelated;
2 To make a three-dimensional space in which vertical and horizontal motion and "natural" left-to-right reading habits would lead an audience to an appreciation and understanding of the logic of life-preserving mechanics;
3 To find a suitable overall form that would communicate the meaning of 1 and 2."[24]

Target Audience
Scientists and the general public.

Understanding Content
Burtin became familiar with the newly discovered complex information about metabolism, coming from many branches of biological, nutritional and chemical research, and worked closely with scientists to understand the chemical reactions he needed to explain through the exhibition.

Idea/Solution
The design solution was rooted in the idea that metabolism is the continuous life-sustaining process, based on the cycles of energy production and use.

Draft Proposals
Burtin and his team sketched more than 200 drawings, created 16 small guide models of separate spheres, and built four scale models of the entire exhibition. With each drawing, model and iteration, the proposed solution found a simpler and clearer way to visually explain the main concepts.

Prototype Design

Visual Translation
Developing the exhibition structure took Burtin nine months. He displayed the metabolic process through a physical representation of a mitochondrion, surrounded by semi-spheres that explained the seven metabolic reactions it accomplishes:

the active transport of glucose;
the synthesis of glycogen;
the synthesis of fat;
the synthesis of protein;
the synthesis of insulin;
muscle contraction; and
the generation of heat.[25]

Burtin used shapes, colors, symbols, electron-micrographic enlargements, scale, light movements and timing to symbolize different parts of the primary structure and explain the function and chemical reactions of a mitochondrion. He achieved such great levels of clarity and accuracy that metabolic processes could be understood with little written explanation.

Image 5.1
Detail of *The Brain* exhibition
for the Upjohn Company, 1960.

CHAPTER 5

Problem

5.1
Defining and Framing

The first step in any design work is to gain an understanding of the situation in order to define or frame the problem. However, as information design problems grow in complexity,[1] this step has become harder to complete. Challenges in information design are well-defined when they are highly framed with a readily tangible solution, and they are ill-defined when their boundaries are ambiguous or unclear and require greater effort to frame and address.[2] According to Alan Siegel and Irene Etzkorn, "one must know what causes a problem before [one] can begin to solve it."[3] Burtin felt that designers "just need a lot of desire to dig into a problem and facts to differentiate one project from another," because each problem presents "a blank slate, where [the designer] must understand the background of a project" before trying to solve it.[4]

Seeking, asking and listening are crucial actions for information designers in the initial stages of a new project to help them identify "a structure, or interpretive frame of reference," which will act as a starting point for generating ideas.[5] When dealing with framed situations, a designer will often determine this structure by analogy to another situation they have encountered in the past. In other words, they define the problem based on whether they have worked on something similar in the past.

Solving unframed information design problems requires a different approach. Close interaction with individuals from other disciplines is needed because, for the designer, extensive learning will be required to identify its structure.[6] The more familiar with a problem-situation a designer is, the more clearly they can determine its structure and key component parts. Similarly, for each of Burtin's projects, he conducted exhaustive investigations to start peeling off layers until the hidden structure and core pieces of the situation were revealed underneath and he had gained a full understanding of it.

In the next section, we discuss the development of *The Brain* exhibition. This project illustrates how Burtin took an apparently framed information design problem—the design of an anatomical exhibition of the brain (what something looks like)—and redefined it when he came to a deeper understanding of the topic. Instead of focusing on anatomical features, Burtin ultimately designed an exhibition that explained brain functions (how something works).

Images 5.2 and 5.3
The Brain exhibition, 1960.

5.2
The Brain Exhibition

Burtin designed *The Brain* exhibition for the Upjohn Company in 1960, for installation at the American Medical Association's annual meeting in Miami Beach, Florida. The exhibition was not an anatomical model, because the main goal was to represent mental functions and the role of time in consciousness and the evolution of thoughts. Explaining "the temporal aspect of brain function" was particularly relevant because scientific research had just revealed that time was the essential factor to understand the steps needed for a thought to emerge.[7] Burtin designed the exhibition to help the average doctor and the general public become acquainted with the most recent scientific discoveries about the human brain and its sensory functions. Viewers would not necessarily need to have anatomical knowledge to understand how the brain works, according to Burtin.[8]

Secondary research on the topic and talks with content experts helped Burtin redefine the problem, and led him to make appropriate decisions based on the project goals rather than on his personal preferences:

> From the beginning of this project, the integration of *all* senses of perception–sight, hearing, smell, taste and touch–in one model was tempting. In the course of research and construction, I had to accept with reluctance the fact that it would be extraordinarily difficult to harmonize this intent with the demands for clear and understandable communication.[9]

Based on his learnings, Burtin determined that the model should restrict "the number of senses, involved in the functional evolution of the thought process, to the two most essential senses–visual and auditory."[10] This decision would prove to be a good one, since viewers could then better understand the internal structures and functioning of these senses.

With moving lights and flashing images, the exhibition visually explained the relationship between consciousness and thought. The viewer's journey began with an audiovisual display of a moment at an opera, projected on a screen. Standing in front of the exhibition, the viewer used headphones for audible information and cues. Inputs coming in through a person's eyes were depicted by two shallow hemispheres or saucer-like structures, and through the ears, by similar saucers placed to the outside and below. These inputs then moved "through elaborate circuitry to various centers of the *Brain* such as the midbrain (the dome-like structure at the bottom), the visual cortices (top, left and right) and the memory cortices (pair of large discs on left and right)."[11]

This experience of sound and sight showed viewers how the human brain works by simulating mental functions that help generate thoughts and judgments. The model itself reacted to these visual and auditory impulses, coming alive to show how a real human brain would process sight and hearing. This audiovisual journey allowed the viewer to experience a feeling similar to "a brief moment at a concert."[12]

> Locations and distances were so arranged that an observer could follow motion and timing of colored light impulses. Selected for a theme was the experience of a singer and her song, both familiar to most people. The sounds and description of the auditory aspects of the experience could be *listened* to over earphones placed near seats around the front of the exhibit, while the motion of green, coded *sound impulses* could be followed visually in the model. The visual aspects of the experience could be seen throughout the performance, as they were cross related to memory flashbacks, and resulted in the final recording of the specific image as red, coded light patterns in memory cortices and midbrain, next to the green patterns of sound.[13]

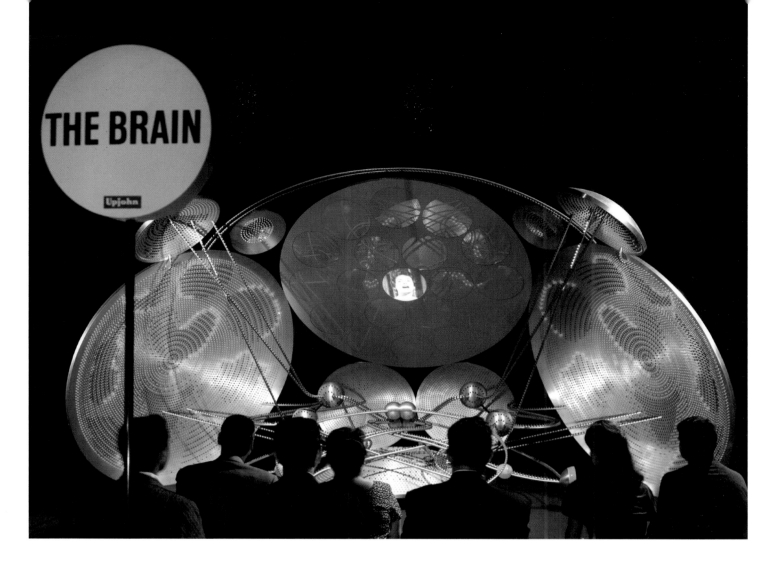

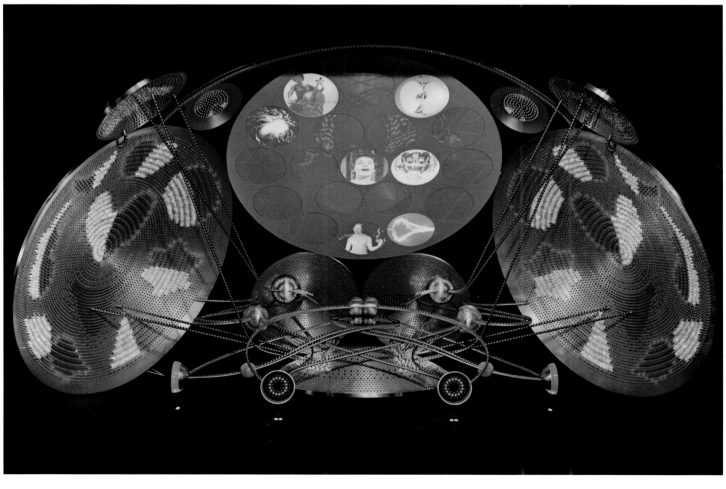

Image 5.4
The Brain exhibition, in construction, 1960.
Work of superb craftsmanship by the Displayers, Inc.

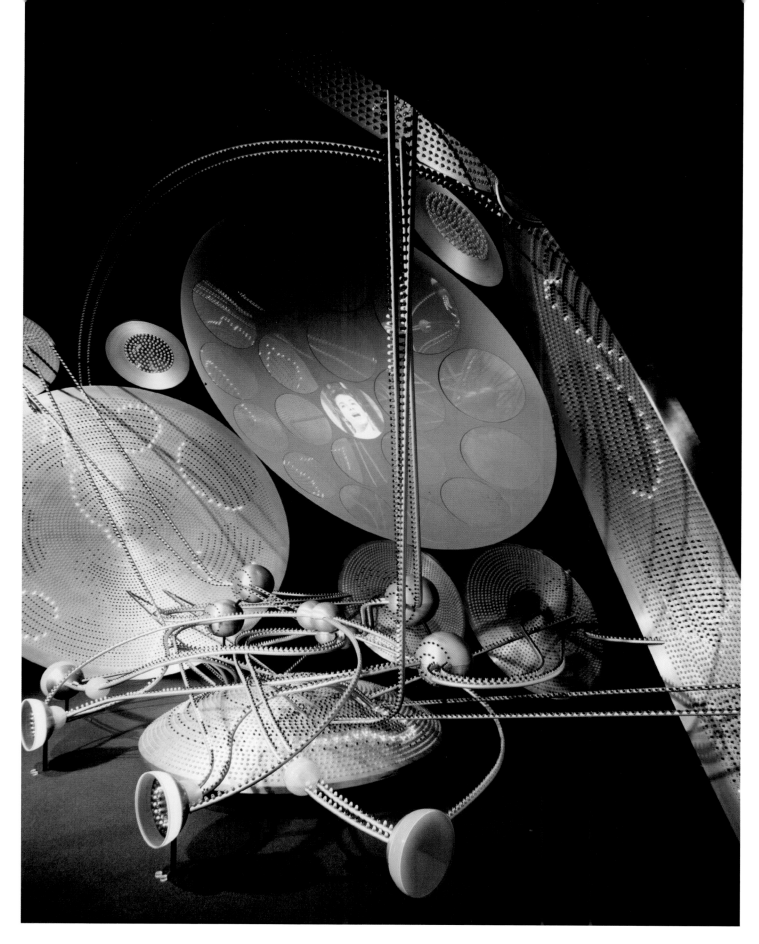

Image 5.5
The Brain exhibition, in construction, 1960.
Lines of small electric lights on concave aluminum discs
serve as the brain centers.

Image 5.6
Will Burtin and Dr. A. Garrard Macleod, Upjohn Company's
Director of Special Projects, survey *The Brain* exhibition, 1960.

Twelve minutes of "model time" was necessary to reveal one second of what we experience in actual time, a time scale of 720 to one. Burtin explained that "within this time limit the demonstration was repeated three times. First came the visual, second the auditory, and then the combination of both sequences." The interplay of sound and sight in the exhibit gave the audience an experience of:

- How the brain receives information
- How it correlates this information
- How it evaluates it
- How it responds to it.

The exhibition was a success because it clearly represented the complicated actions of the brain as the well-defined and understandable steps of a process. The scale of the model, its materials and how the three-dimensional space depicted time demonstrated, Burtin wrote, "the complexities of simultaneous interrelations between chemistry, functioning purposes and resulting organic forms." Overall, the exhibition helped viewers understand "the growth of new knowledge" about the brain's operational principles and functions that emerged largely in the 1950s. A doctor said that the exhibition was "fascinating, and so well-conceived that it makes neuro-anatomy and physiology comprehensible." Following Burtin's rationale to represent abstract concepts as 3D models, schools and universities built smaller-sized models of their own drawings about the brain and its functions.

The Brain exhibition was featured on television and seen by millions of Americans. It traveled nationally to many American cities and internationally to Germany, Italy, France, the Netherlands, Belgium and England (see chapter 9) and was subsequently featured in televised lectures, motion pictures and many publications throughout the world.

Burtin also designed a brochure, *A Moment at a Concert*, to reinforce and expand the information presented in the exhibition. The brochure was square (8.5 × 8.5 in.) and combined photography from *The Brain* exhibition with diagrams and textual explanations about the neurophysiological events of the brain during a brief moment at a concert, focusing on sight and hearing. (see images 5.7 to 5.13.)

The brochure presented important developments about the nervous system functions, including visual explanations of the visual and auditory mechanisms, how the brain records memories, and the centrencephalic system. For example, page 3 illustrated changes in the irides in response to light stimuli of different intensity: initial eye dilation (outer circle of blue dots), eye contraction (inner ring of blue dots), right amount of light for optimum clarity of vision (white dots). (see image 5.9.)

Image 5.7
Cover, *A Moment at a Concert* brochure, 1961.

Images 5.8 and 5.9
Inside pages, *A Moment at a Concert* brochure.

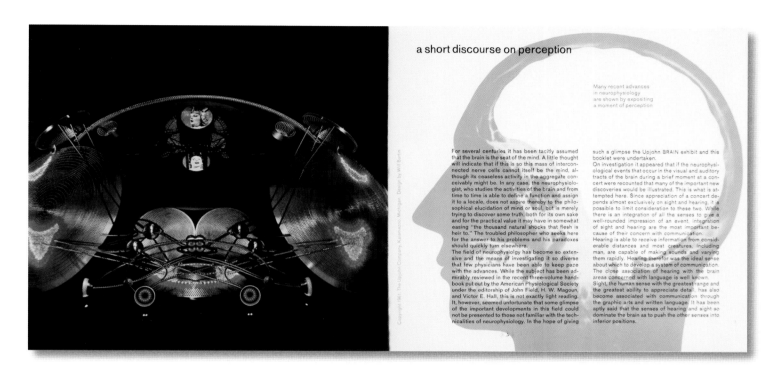

a short discourse on perception

Many recent advances
in neurophysiology
are shown by expositing
a moment of perception

For several centuries it has been tacitly assumed that the brain is the seat of the mind. A little thought will indicate that if this is so this mass of interconnected nerve cells cannot itself be the mind, although its ceaseless activity in the aggregate conceivably might be. In any case, the neurophysiologist, who studies the activities of the brain and from time to time is able to define a function and assign it to a locale, does not aspire thereby to the philosophical elucidation of mind or soul, but is merely trying to discover some truth, both for its own sake and for the practical value it may have in somewhat easing "the thousand natural shocks that flesh is heir to." The troubled philosopher who seeks here for the answer to his problems and his paradoxes should quickly turn elsewhere.

The field of neurophysiology has become so extensive and the means of investigating it so diverse that few physicians have been able to keep pace with the advances. While the subject has been admirably reviewed in the recent three-volume handbook put out by the American Physiological Society under the editorship of John Field, H. W. Magoun, and Victor E. Hall, this is not exactly light reading. It, however, seemed unfortunate that some glimpse of the important developments in this field could not be presented to those not familiar with the technicalities of neurophysiology. In the hope of giving such a glimpse the Upjohn BRAIN exhibit and this booklet were undertaken.

On investigation it appeared that if the neurophysiological events that occur in the visual and auditory tracts of the brain during a brief moment at a concert were recounted that many of the important new discoveries would be illustrated. This is what is attempted here. Since appreciation of a concert depends almost exclusively on sight and hearing, it is possible to limit consideration to these two. While there is an integration of all the senses to give a well-rounded impression of an event, integration of sight and hearing are the most important because of their concern with communication.

Hearing is able to receive information from considerable distances and most creatures, including man, are capable of making sounds and varying them rapidly. Hearing therefor was the ideal sense about which to develop a system of communication. The close association of hearing with the brain areas concerned with language is well known.

Sight, the human sense with the greatest range and the greatest ability to appreciate detail, has also become associated with communication through the graphic arts and written language. It has been aptly said that the senses of hearing and sight so dominate the brain as to push the other senses into inferior positions.

Copyright 1961, The Upjohn Company, Kalamazoo, Michigan. Design by Will Burtin.

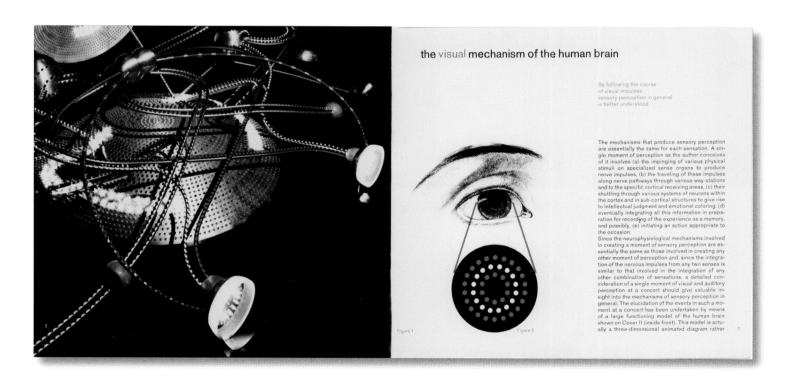

the visual mechanism of the human brain

By following the course
of visual impulses
sensory perception in general
is better understood

The mechanisms that produce sensory perception are essentially the same for each sensation. A single moment of perception as the author conceives of it involves (a) the impinging of various physical stimuli on specialized sense organs to produce nerve impulses, (b) the traveling of these impulses along nerve pathways through various way-stations and to the specific cortical receiving areas, (c) their shuttling through various systems of neurons within the cortex and in sub-cortical structures to give rise to intellectual judgment and emotional coloring, (d) eventually integrating all this information in preparation for recording of the experience as a memory, and possibly, (e) initiating an action appropriate to the occasion.

Since the neurophysiological mechanisms involved in creating a moment of sensory perception are essentially the same as those involved in creating any other moment of perception and, since the integration of the nervous impulses from any two senses is similar to that involved in the integration of any other combination of sensations, a detailed consideration of a single moment of visual and auditory perception at a concert should give valuable insight into the mechanisms of sensory perception in general. The elucidation of the events in such a moment at a concert has been undertaken by means of a large functioning model of the human brain shown on Cover II (inside front). This model is actually a three-dimensional animated diagram rather

Figure 1   Figure 2

Images 5.10 and 5.11
Inside pages, *A Moment at a Concert* brochure.

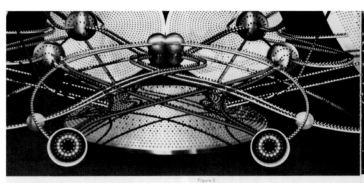

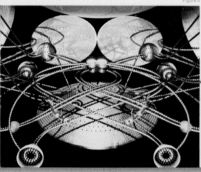
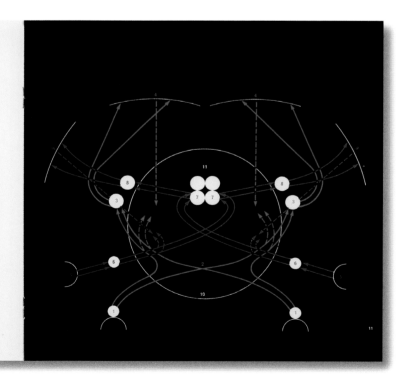

Images 5.12 and 5.13
Inside pages, *A Moment at a Concert* brochure.

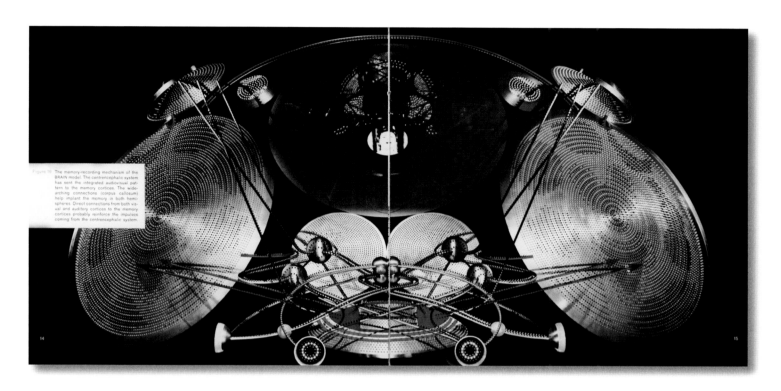

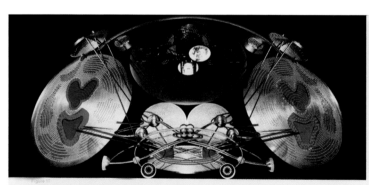

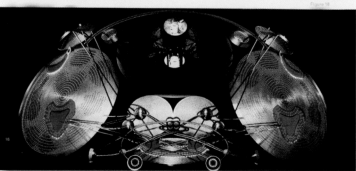

subcortical structures and psychopharmacology

The subcortical structures
involved in awareness and emotion
are important in
the field of psychopharmacology

The centrencephalic system

In the course of this discussion a great deal has been said about the centrencephalic system. This term has been used because it is relatively concise and suggestive in much the same manner that Wilder Penfield has used it in his discussion of the extremely important observations on brain function in conscious patients during operations for temporal lobe epilepsy. The centrencephalic system has now been quite clearly identified with the anatomical structures known for many years as the reticular formation in the regions of the thalamus and midbrain. Many of the important functions of this system have been elucidated by the experimental work of H. W. Magoun, Herbert Jasper and many others. Unfortunately, the many extremely interesting experimental observations that have been made on this structure cannot be reviewed here in detail. However, some of the general conclusions, which at the current state of knowledge seem to be justified, can be pointed out.

The structure itself may be described as a very complex interconnecting mass of neurons packed in and around the more sharply-defined structures of the midbrain and the diencephalon. Functionally it may be divided roughly into at least two systems –the descending reticular system and the ascending reticular activating system.

The descending reticular system's function seems to be primarily inhibitory on certain of the motor neurons in the spinal cord. It seems to be concerned with the reciprocal inhibitions which are needed for the smooth performance of any action. For instance, when a baseball player swings his bat at a ball, it is the coordinating function of the descending reticular system to inhibit those muscle groups which might otherwise impede the swing. Descending or centrifugal impulses from the reticular system also have an important influence on afferent sensory impulses. This influence also seems to be predominantly inhibitory. Experimental stimulation of the reticular system attenuates the impulses coming from the various sense organs. It

NOTES

1 Sheila Pontis, *Making Sense of Field Research:
   A Practical Guide for Information Designers*
   (Oxfordshire, UK: Routledge, 2018).

2 Rowan Conway, Jeff Masters and Jake Thorold,
   "From Design Thinking to Systems Change"
   (London: RSA Action and Research Centre, July 2017),
   https://www.thersa.org/globalassets/pdfs/reports/rsa_from-
   design-thinking-to-system-change-report.pdf.

3 Alan Siegel and Irene Etzkorn, *Simple: Conquering the Crisis
   of Complexity* (New York: Twelve, 2013), 13.

4 Will Burtin, "Theory of Design Course Lectures"
   (Lecture 1, February 20, 1947), 1, Will Burtin Papers, 96.7,
   Cary Graphic Design Archive, RIT

5 Donald A. Schön in Mary M. Kennedy, "Inexact Sciences:
   Professional Education and the Development of Expertise,"
   Review of Research in Education, 14, no. 1 (January 1987): 148.

6 Pontis, *Making Sense*.

7 Burtin, "Brain, correspondence" (unpublished draft for
   Industrial Design vol. 7 no. 8, August 1960), 4,
   Will Burtin Papers, 12.3–12.4,
   Cary Graphic Design Archive, RIT.

8 Burtin, "Observations on the Development of the
   Brain Model" (unpublished manuscript, April 10, 1960),
   Will Burtin Papers, 12.3, Cary Graphic Design Archive, RIT.

9 Burtin, "Reflections on Graphic Design"
   (unpublished manuscript, 1966), 10, Will Burtin Papers, 93.5,
   Cary Graphic Design Archive, RIT.

10 Burtin, "Observations," 3.

11 R. Roger Remington and Robert S.P. Fripp,
   Design and Science: The Life and Work of Will Burtin
   (Hampshire, UK: Lund Humphries, 2007), 89.

12 *Moment at a Concert*, exhibition brochure
   (Kalamazoo, MI: Upjohn, 1961), 1, Will Burtin Papers, 67.5–67.6,
   Cary Graphic Design Archive, RIT.

13 Burtin, "Reflections," 14.

14 Ibid.

15 Remington and Fripp, *Design and Science*, 89.

16 Burtin, "Observations," 2.

17 Ibid.

18 Remington and Fripp, *Design and Science*, 93.

19 Burtin, "Observations."

20 *A Moment*.

21 Burtin, "Reflections," 14.

22 Burtin, "Observations," 2.

23 Burtin, "Reflections," 14.

24 Burtin, "Observations," 2.

25 Burtin, "Observations," 3.

26 *A Moment*, 3–4.

27 Burtin, "Observations," 4.

5.3
Process Box 2
Case Study 2: *The Brain* **Exhibition (1960)**

Conceptual Design

Understanding and Framing the Problem
The challenge was to provide an experience that tied together many fields of knowledge and explained many diverse components, from psycho-mechanical to chemical. "The design problem was defined in the direction of searching for a type of visual-auditory demonstration, which would point out the order by which the main product of the brain, a thought, evolves."[21] Working with Dr. A. Garrard Macleod, a scientist from Upjohn, Burtin came to the conclusion that concerns about anatomical details were a barrier to helping the audience fully understand the "operational principles on which consciousness–the essential product of the brain–is based."[22]

Target Audience
Scientists and the general public.

Understanding Content
Burtin made sense of the workings of the brain through scientific research, working in collaboration with design and scientific teams. He gained an understanding of medical theory and practice, and manufacturing technology, and became familiar with the anatomical relationship of brain components. "At a relatively early stage of the design investigation, it became evident that to remain understandable, the form of this demonstration should not be based on the anatomical geography of the organ, but perhaps on the sequential order of the thinking process itself."[23]

Idea/Solution
As a solution, Burtin proposed the creation of a visual teaching aid that would translate the "complex processes and sensations [of the human brain] into understandable images."[24]

Draft Proposals
Burtin proposed a life-sized, time-space model that would portray and thus explain the interlocking actions of sight and hearing, two of the more prominent sensory mechanisms in the brain. "The first model was constructed in the fall of 1958, to show what a conceptual image of the brain functions would be like if compared with conventional anatomical models. This model served as a starting point for subsequent studies."[25]

Prototype Design

Visual Translation
It took nearly one year to design and execute the finished brain model, which was an evolution from the initial model. Burtin's team built three small-scale models; produced more than 100 drawings of parts, wiring diagrams and floor plans; and developed 12 sketch models, six of which became additional side exhibitions. The final model was "a three-dimensional animated diagram rather than a realistic anatomic representation."[26] To represent brain functions, Burtin utilized shapes (shallow hemispheres, tubes), colors (green for sound, red for vision), color transparencies, sounds and materials. "The addition of a 'consciousness screen' in the center of the exhibit" ensured "a logical and clear relationship between the mechanics and the representational nature of thinking."[27]

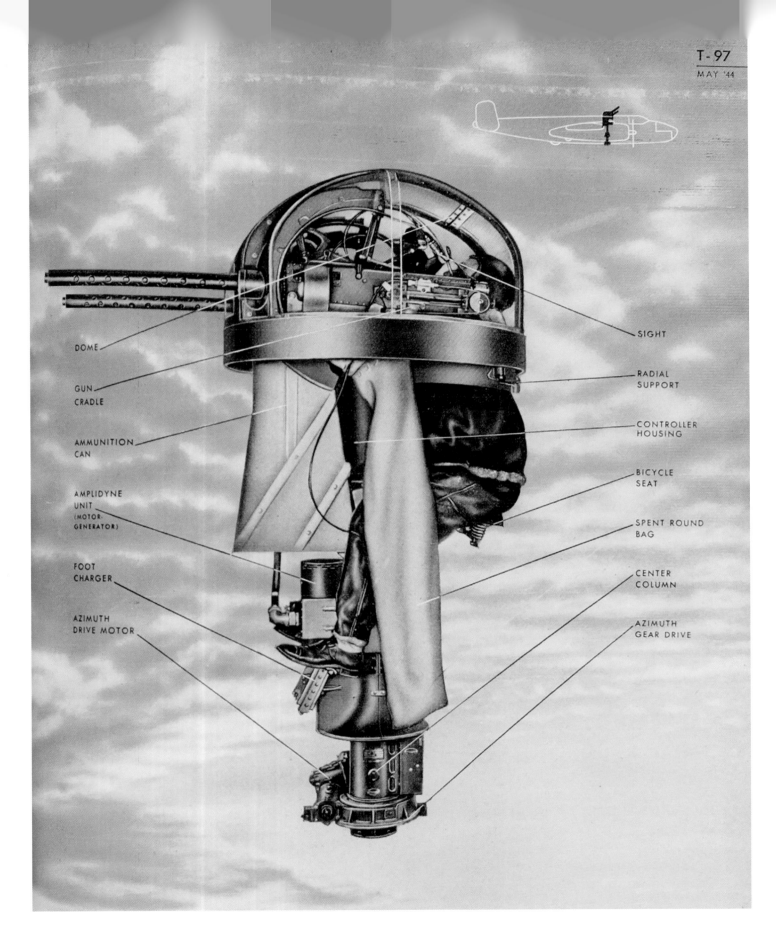

SIGHT

DOME

RADIAL
SUPPORT

GUN
CRADLE

CONTROLLER
HOUSING

AMMUNITION
CAN

BICYCLE
SEAT

AMPLIDYNE
UNIT
(MOTOR-
GENERATOR)

SPENT ROUND
BAG

FOOT
CHARGER

CENTER
COLUMN

AZIMUTH
DRIVE MOTOR

AZIMUTH
GEAR DRIVE

Image 6.1
Diagram from *This is Your Gun* manual explaining the parts
of The Bendix Upper Turret, an all-electric gun used in the
upper area of the B-25 Mitchell bomber, 1944.

Audience

6.1
A Human-Centered Process

Up to this point, we have clarified the notion of an information design goal and discussed defining and framing a design problem. Before moving forward in the process, we must now consider the role of the audience in the design process, since understanding the audience is as important as understanding the problem. Designers must determine who the audience is early on, and gain a thorough understanding of its needs and behaviors. Will Burtin felt that the "designer should see his craft as the link *between* the realm of ideas and the reality of people. Understanding of both is his highest challenge and biggest reward."[1]

Learning about an audience and what is important to it determines which facts are relevant and which are superfluous, which should be presented as written word and which should be translated into visual forms. Burtin called this "the work of men who have the courage to do what they know is right" for the audience, "and not because it is convenient for technical or esthetic reasons."[2]

Today, "Organizing the design process around users is a vital vein of contemporary practice"[3] and is often described as a human-centered approach. By studying and gaining an understanding of the intended audience, information designers can develop visual and educational "aids that will make maximum use of a person's abilities."[4] Designers need to learn the attributes of their audience, both *demographic* (age, gender, profession, geographic location, education) and *psychographic* (personality, values, attitudes, interests, lifestyles). The greater their familiarity with their audience, the more informed their design decisions will be and the more likely their solutions will meet the needs of their audience.

Image 6.2
Will Burtin during World
War II, assigned to Office of
Strategic Services, 1943.

When working on framed challenges, designers can use secondary research and rely on their previous experience, background knowledge and overall project know-how. However, as design challenges become more unframed, "personal experience and knowledge alone aren't enough" for a designer to learn about the audience and create effective solutions.[5] In these cases, a more thorough understanding of the problem and the audience is needed, so some form of primary research is necessary to gather insights. Information designers frequently use market research and usability testing methods. In addition, they also are increasingly adopting ethnographic research approaches, where the audience is studied in its own environment, and people's behavior can be observed in everyday practices. Some of these methods are contextual interviews, observations, co-creation workshops, task analysis, and cultural probes.[6] Variations of these methods can be used, depending on the budget, time and complexity of each project.[7]

A distinctive characteristic of Burtin's scientific approach was its strong focus on the audience and understanding its needs through ethnographic research. His designs were conceived with the intended user in mind. For example, Burtin's gunnery training manuals, designed during World War II, helped young recruits learn how to use defensive Air Force armaments. For these manuals, Burtin used a form of ethnographic research commonly used today by information designers:[8] the "walk a mile in your customer's shoes" method. He literally put himself into the intended users' shoes in order to experience the situations they were dealing with. In the process, he learned how to use combat gunnery.

6.2
Gunner's Information File Project

In 1943, Burtin volunteered for the US military service. By 1944, the US Army Air Force (USAAF) was seeking a more effective means of training Air Force gunners how to operate the defensive gunnery on various bombers. Based in Washington DC, Burtin was assigned to the Office of Strategic Services (OSS, Intelligence and Special Operations) to address this problem and soon was leading a team of designers, photographers and writers, including Max Gschwind, Lawrence Lessing, Frank Zachary, William Golden, Tobias Moss, Dong Kingman, Russell Lynes, Saul Steinberg and Harold Ross.

The output was the *Gunner's Information File* project, four loose-leaf gunnery manuals for young American enlistees in the US Army Air Force: *Position Firing Against Fighters Attacking on the Curve of Pursuit* (May 1944), *This is Your Gun* (May 1944), *Gunnery in the B-29* (August 1944) and *Gunnery in the A-26* (November 1944). Burtin's goal when designing these manuals was first to assess the complex, largely invisible and changing factors involved in the project, and then to create visuals that would expand the text and make the information comprehensible, usable and second nature to gunners. What made this project more challenging than most was that the manuals' intended users had no previous knowledge of how to use a gun or be a gunner. The new recruits needed to learn how to quickly calculate critical variables such as multi-factorial vectors of airspeed, wind speed, range, trajectory and attack angle.

To thoroughly understand these actions, Burtin became a gunner himself, working in collaboration with the USAAF Board, the USAAF School of Applied Tactics, the Second Air Force and the USAAF Training Command. Burtin took parachute training and was ordered aloft several times to get familiar with the challenges faced by recruits. In this way, he was able to empathize with the trainees, understand what they were doing, and identify the hardest parts of the process. "There are so many issues involved in the training," he wrote, "that it is not surprising that pilots and aerial gunners need between 8 and 13 months until they are ready for the final test: combat."[9]

Once Burtin had created a prototype, it was field-tested for optimum legibility and understanding. The resulting manuals were all the same format (11 × 8.5 in.) and combined textual information with detailed visual explanations and diagrams, primarily showing how to use guns during combat. The manuals also covered abstract concepts, like bullet trajectory, both from an objective standpoint and from the perspective of a gunner. The visuals clearly showed what a situation would look like to a gunner, and what would actually be happening at the same time in the air. For Burtin, an attack was "as simple as [a] picture indicates."[10] The clarity of his thought is reflected in each page of the manuals.

In order to engage the recruits and keep them interested, Burtin introduced basic concepts and explanations, according to their needs and preferences. "The message had to be direct and swiftly to the point"[11] because the competencies learned from these manuals would be essential at any time, in any weather and in any combat situation. However, Burtin also acknowledged with sensitivity the complexity of his audience:

> No necessity was felt to talk down to the audience, as many war manuals did. Many manuals attempted to divert men's minds from a natural revulsion to killing or being killed by sugarcoating the message, clowning or employing comic-strip techniques. But these only served to warp relationships between the soldier and his job. He was engaged in a serious business in which his life might someday depend on the swift functioning of his knowledge and equipment. He deserved dignified treatment and the clearest possible statement offsets.[12]

The manuals presented a holistic story: Rather than simply providing instructions for how to use the guns of each specific plane, they also included relevant information and guidance to enhance the whole experience of becoming a gunner. This information helped airmen to understand and learn complex skills, and then to put their newly acquired knowledge into practice.

Burtin's design solution succeeded in helping American enlistees better comprehend how to use aerial guns and "by the use of these visual aids and principles, training time for aerial gunners was cut exactly in half, from twelve weeks to six."[13] Burtin and Lawrence Lessing evaluated the manuals in 1948: "As happens whenever all the elements of a design are recognized, studied and brought coherently together, the result is hardly ever unpleasing to the eye–indeed, it achieves a certain beauty of clear statement–and is effective in its purpose."[14]

Gunnery in the A-26 Manual, November 1944

The manual for the A-26 described the airplane's key features and the characteristics of new gunnery equipment, the gunner's compartment, how to adjust his sight to use the periscope, specifics on how to use the guns when in combat, steps to get ready for a mission and how to harmonize the airplane (unify all the technical systems). At the end of the manual, to ensure that all the necessary protocols had been followed correctly, four checklists were included, one for each step in the experience: pre-flight, in air, before landing and post flight. In the manual, this information was logically presented in seven sequential chapters:

- The A-26 and its guns
- The Gunners Compartment and its Switches
- Sight
- The A-26 in Combat
- Getting Ready for the Mission
- Harmonization of the A-26
- Check Lists

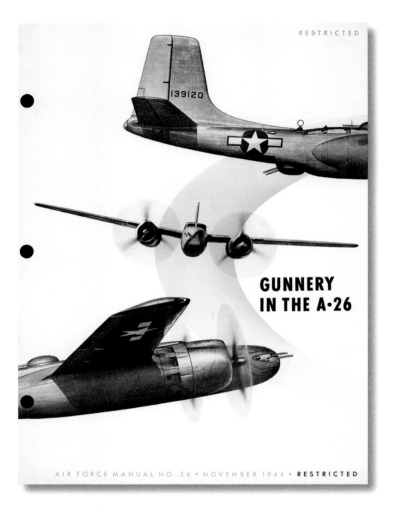

Image 6.4
Inside pages, *Gunnery in the A-26* manual.

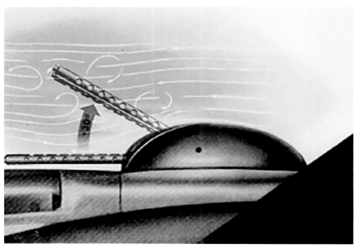

Image 6.5
Inside pages, *Gunnery in the A-26* manual.
Operations of a gun sight.

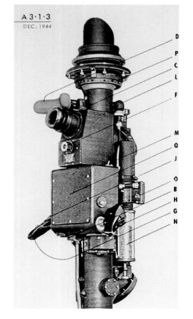

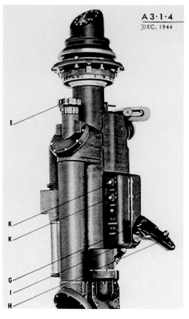

Image 6.6
Inside pages, *Gunnery in the A-26* manual.
Harmonization of the A-26 airplane.

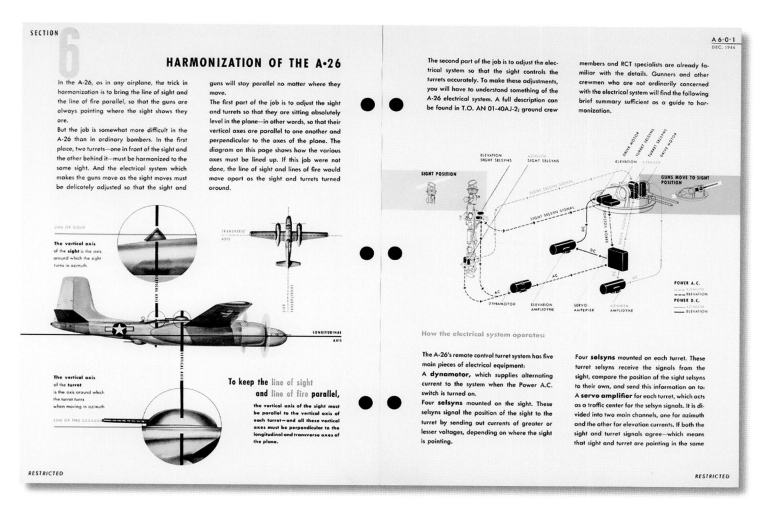

HARMONIZATION OF THE A-26

A 6·0·1
DEC. 1944

In the A-26, as in any airplane, the trick in harmonization is to bring the line of sight and the line of fire parallel, so that the guns are always pointing where the sight shows they are.

But the job is somewhat more difficult in the A-26 than in ordinary bombers. In the first place, two turrets—one in front of the sight and the other behind it—must be harmonized to the same sight. And the electrical system which makes the guns move as the sight moves must be delicately adjusted so that the sight and

guns will stay parallel no matter where they move.

The first part of the job is to adjust the sight and turrets so that they are sitting absolutely level in the plane—in other words, so that their vertical axes are parallel to one another and perpendicular to the axes of the plane. The diagram on this page shows how the various axes must be lined up. If this job were not done, the line of sight and lines of fire would move apart as the sight and turrets turned around.

The second part of the job is to adjust the electrical system so that the sight controls the turrets accurately. To make these adjustments, you will have to understand something of the A-26 electrical system. A full description can be found in T.O. AN 01-40AJ-2; ground crew members and RCT specialists are already familiar with the details. Gunners and other crewmen who are not ordinarily concerned with the electrical system will find the following brief summary sufficient as a guide to harmonization.

LINE OF SIGHT

The vertical axis of the **sight** is the axis around which the sight turns in azimuth.

TRANSVERSE AXIS

LONGITUDINAL AXIS

The vertical axis of the **turret** is the axis around which the turret turns when moving in azimuth.

LINE OF FIRE

To keep the line of sight **and** line of fire **parallel,** the vertical axis of the sight must be parallel to the vertical axis of each turret—and all these vertical axes must be perpendicular to the longitudinal and transverse axes of the plane.

How the electrical system operates:

The A-26's remote control turret system has five main pieces of electrical equipment:

A **dynamotor,** which supplies alternating current to the system when the Power A.C. switch is turned on.

Four **selsyns** mounted on the sight. These selsyns signal the position of the sight to the turret by sending out currents of greater or lesser voltages, depending on where the sight is pointing.

Four **selsyns** mounted on each turret. These turret selsyns receive the signals from the sight, compare the position of the sight selsyns to their own, and send this information on to:

A **servo amplifier** for each turret, which acts as a traffic center for the selsyn signals. It is divided into two main channels, one for azimuth and the other for elevation currents. If both the sight and turret signals agree—which means that sight and turret are pointing in the same

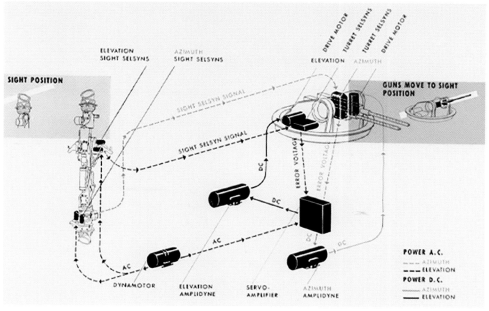

Gunnery in the B-29 Manual, August 1944

This training manual is the most notable of the series. Explanatory graphics accompany wide columns of excessively leaded sans-serif text type to enhance readability. The diagrammatic and typographic components are arranged in a geometric fashion that creates both a functional hierarchy and an easy flow to the page. The trainee's eye was caught with each diagram, and then moved into the accompanying text.

Learning the complexity of the B-29 guns was a major aspect of this training. The overall priority, however, was for the gunner to become familiar with the functionalities of the remote-control system, which connected the four gun turrets and the one in the tail by a hydraulic tracker system. He also had to learn loading, dismantling and servicing the guns. Instruction in the manual is sequenced, becoming increasingly complex as the learner progresses through it.

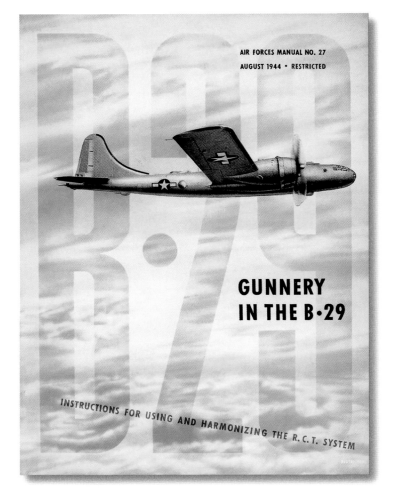

AIR FORCES MANUAL NO. 27

AUGUST 1944 • RESTRICTED

**GUNNERY
IN THE B•29**

INSTRUCTIONS FOR USING AND HARMONIZING THE R. C. T. SYSTEM

Image 6.8
Inside pages, *Gunnery in the B-29* manual.

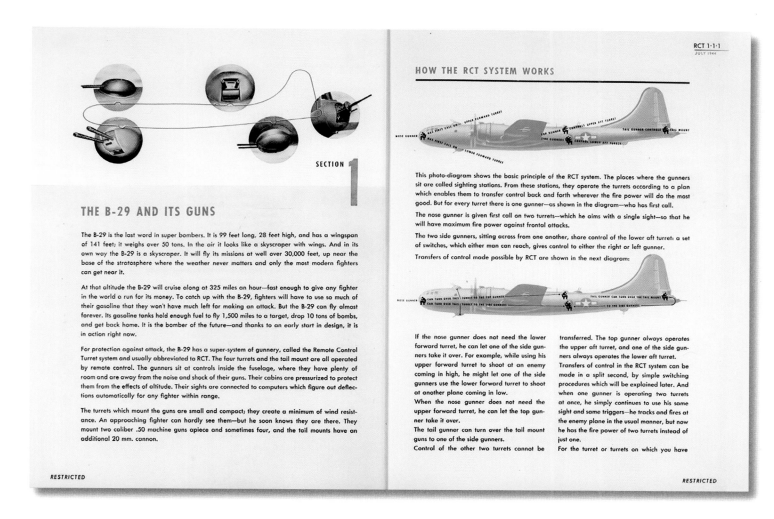

SECTION 1

THE B-29 AND ITS GUNS

The B-29 is the last word in super bombers. It is 99 feet long, 28 feet high, and has a wingspan of 141 feet; it weighs over 50 tons. In the air it looks like a skyscraper with wings. And in its own way the B-29 is a skyscraper. It will fly its missions at well over 30,000 feet, up near the base of the stratosphere where the weather never matters and only the most modern fighters can get near it.

At that altitude the B-29 will cruise along at 325 miles an hour—fast enough to give any fighter in the world a run for its money. To catch up with the B-29, fighters will have to use so much of their gasoline that they won't have much left for making an attack. But the B-29 can fly almost forever. Its gasoline tanks hold enough fuel to fly 1,500 miles to a target, drop 10 tons of bombs, and get back home. It is the bomber of the future—and thanks to an early start in design, it is in action right now.

For protection against attack, the B-29 has a super-system of gunnery, called the Remote Control Turret system and usually abbreviated to RCT. The four turrets and the tail mount are all operated by remote control. The gunners sit at controls inside the fuselage, where they have plenty of room and are away from the noise and shock of their guns. Their cabins are pressurized to protect them from the effects of altitude. Their sights are connected to computers which figure out deflections automatically for any fighter within range.

The turrets which mount the guns are small and compact; they create a minimum of wind resistance. An approaching fighter can hardly see them—but he soon knows they are there. They mount two caliber .50 machine guns apiece and sometimes four, and the tail mounts have an additional 20 mm. cannon.

HOW THE RCT SYSTEM WORKS

This photo-diagram shows the basic principle of the RCT system. The places where the gunners sit are called sighting stations. From these stations, they operate the turrets according to a plan which enables them to transfer control back and forth wherever the fire power will do the most good. But for every turret there is one gunner—as shown in the diagram—who has first call.

The nose gunner is given first call on two turrets—which he aims with a single sight—so that he will have maximum fire power against frontal attacks.

The two side gunners, sitting across from one another, share control of the lower aft turret: a set of switches, which either man can reach, gives control to either the right or left gunner.

Transfers of control made possible by RCT are shown in the next diagram:

If the nose gunner does not need the lower forward turret, he can let one of the side gunners take it over. For example, while using his upper forward turret to shoot at an enemy coming in high, he might let one of the side gunners use the lower forward turret to shoot at another plane coming in low.

When the nose gunner does not need the upper forward turret, he can let the top gunner take it over.

The tail gunner can turn over the tail mount guns to one of the side gunners.

Control of the other two turrets cannot be transferred. The top gunner always operates the upper aft turret, and one of the side gunners always operates the lower aft turret.

Transfers of control in the RCT system can be made in a split second, by simple switching procedures which will be explained later. And when one gunner is operating two turrets at once, he simply continues to use his same sight and same triggers—he tracks and fires at the enemy plane in the usual manner, but now he has the fire power of two turrets instead of just one.

For the turret or turrets on which you have

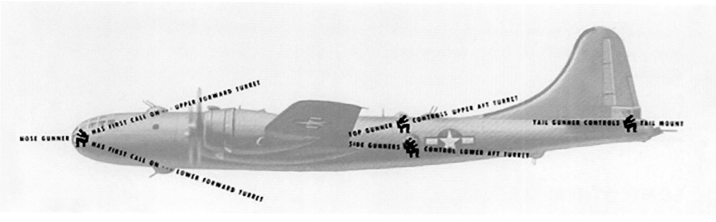

Image 6.9
Inside pages, *Gunnery in the B-29* manual.

Image 6.10
Inside pages, *Gunnery in the B-29* manual.

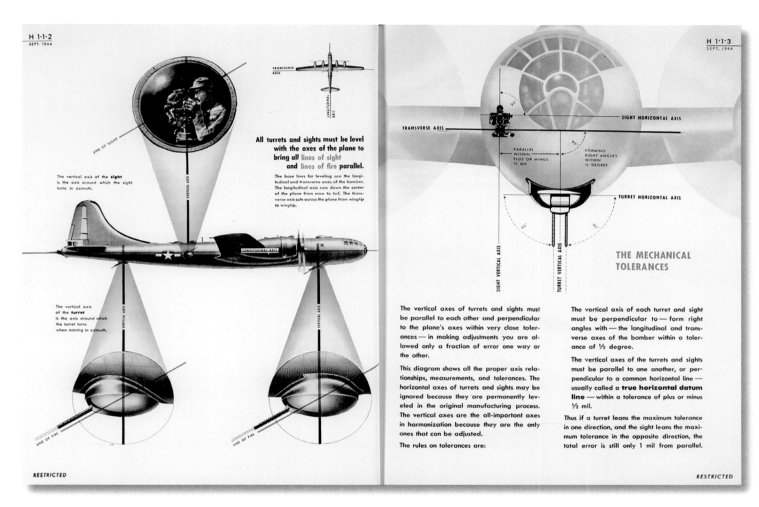

TRANSVERSE AXIS

LINE OF SIGHT

All turrets and sights must be level with the axes of the plane to bring all lines of sight and lines of fire parallel.

The base lines for leveling are the longitudinal and transverse axes of the bomber. The longitudinal axis runs down the center of the plane from nose to tail. The transverse axis cuts across the plane from wingtip to wingtip.

The vertical axis of the **sight** is the axis around which the sight turns in azimuth.

VERTICAL AXIS

The vertical axis of the **turret** is the axis around which the turret turns when moving in azimuth.

VERTICAL AXIS

VERTICAL AXIS

LINE OF FIRE

LINE OF FIRE

RESTRICTED

TRANSVERSE AXIS

SIGHT HORIZONTAL AXIS

PARALLEL WITHIN PLUS OR MINUS ½ MIL

FORMING RIGHT ANGLES WITHIN ½ DEGREE

TURRET HORIZONTAL AXIS

SIGHT VERTICAL AXIS

TURRET VERTICAL AXIS

THE MECHANICAL TOLERANCES

The vertical axes of turrets and sights must be parallel to each other and perpendicular to the plane's axes within very close tolerances — in making adjustments you are allowed only a fraction of error one way or the other.

This diagram shows all the proper axis relationships, measurements, and tolerances. The horizontal axes of turrets and sights may be ignored because they are permanently leveled in the original manufacturing process. The vertical axes are the all-important axes in harmonization because they are the only ones that can be adjusted.

The rules on tolerances are:

The vertical axis of each turret and sight must be perpendicular to — form right angles with — the longitudinal and transverse axes of the bomber within a tolerance of ½ degree.

The vertical axes of the turrets and sights must be parallel to one another, or perpendicular to a common horizontal line — usually called a **true horizontal datum line** — within a tolerance of plus or minus ½ mil.

Thus if a turret leans the maximum tolerance in one direction, and the sight leans the maximum tolerance in the opposite direction, the total error is still only 1 mil from parallel.

RESTRICTED

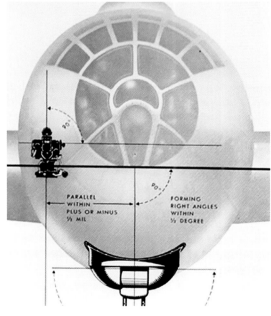

PARALLEL WITHIN PLUS OR MINUS ½ MIL

FORMING RIGHT ANGLES WITHIN ½ DEGREE

Position Firing Manual, May 1944

This manual was titled, *Position Firing Against Fighters Attacking on the Curve of Pursuit*. Primarily through easy-to-read diagrams showing airplane battle positions, gunners were shown detailed techniques for firing at enemy aircraft that would be pursuing them. In order to communicate the space-time-motion relationship, Burtin approached the problem in three steps:

> First, the area around the bomber was laid out on a one-dimensional plane using color to illuminate its basic measurements. Then the one-dimensional changed into the three-dimensional by the projection of imaginary, transparent cones in space. Finally, the gunner was shown how the angle measurements of these cones were carried forward and backward in space and measured with the rings of his gun sight.[15]

POSITION FIRING

SECTION OF THE GUNNER'S INFORMATION FILE

AIR FORCES MANUAL No. 20 · MAY 1944 ·

RESTRICTED

Image 6.12
Inside pages, *Position Firing* manual.

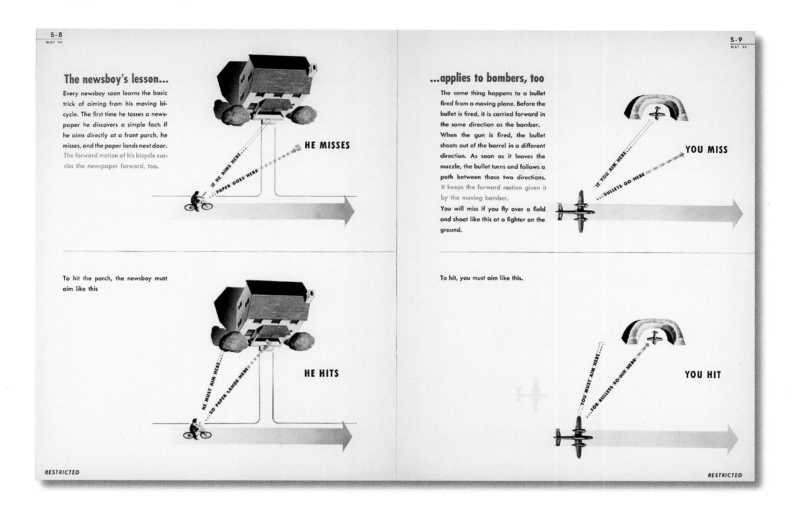

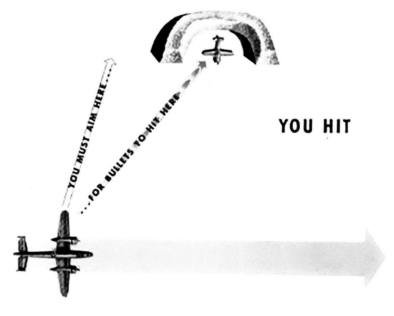

YOU HIT

Image 6.13
Inside pages, *Position Firing* manual.

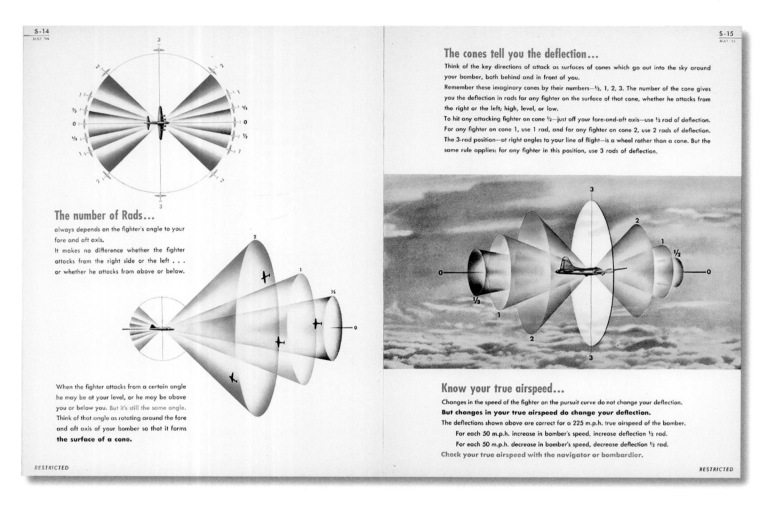

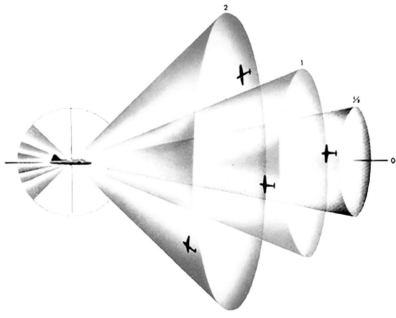

Image 6.14
Inside pages, *Position Firing* manual.

Pursuit curve attack from the side.

Pursuit curve attack from the nose.

Pursuit curve attack from the tail.

Pursuit curve attack from overhead.

RESTRICTED

Fighters will try anything . . .

They may come in from the side, the nose, or the tail, or even from overhead. But all these attacks have one thing in common, as shown on the opposite page. No matter from what direction the fighter approaches, he must maneuver into a position where he can get his guns bearing on you.

To keep them bearing he must fly a pursuit curve.

That is the part of the attack where he is really dangerous to you,
and fortunately, that's where Position Firing makes him easiest for you to hit.

Remember, you are moving too . . .

This is not as self-evident as it seems, because when you are flying in a bomber, you're rarely conscious of your own motion.

But the simple fact that you are moving at high speed is of the greatest importance in learning where to aim.

Believe it or not—

Your bullets do not go where you point your gun.

RESTRICTED

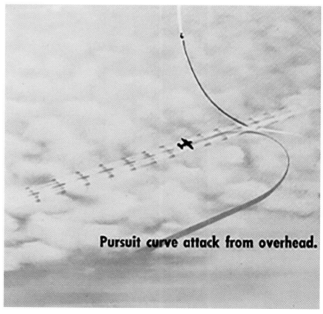

Pursuit curve attack from overhead.

This is Your Gun Manual, May 1944

This manual detailed the operation and maintenance of the caliber .50 Browning machine gun, as well as brief instructions for the caliber .30 machine gun and caliber .45 automatic pistol. The introductory page, written by US Army General Henry H. "Hap" Arnold, introduces the contents of the training manual: the workings of the machine gun, the rules of position firing, the kinds of sights used and the operation of a turret. He concludes by stressing, "There is no unnecessary theory in this book, or in the way your instructors will teach you these facts. Everything is practical; you will use every bit of it. It is your round trip ticket into combat."[16]

Image 6.16
Inside pages, *This is Your Gun* manual.

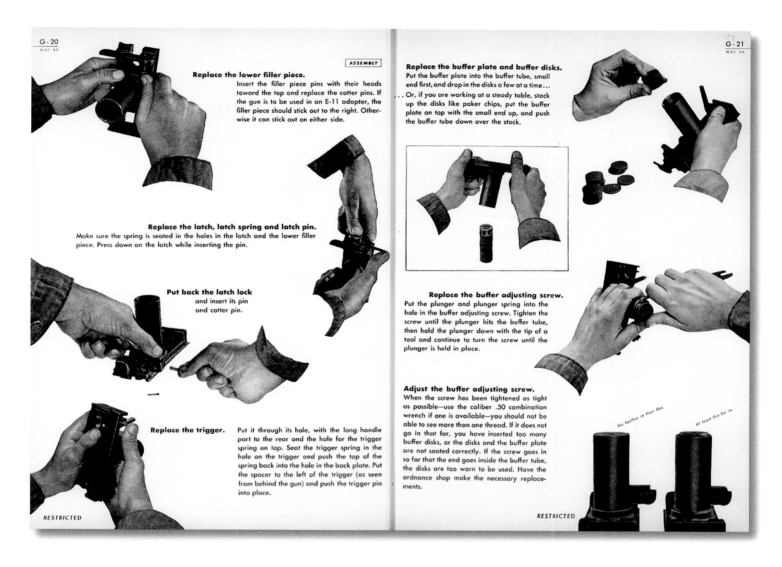

ASSEMBLY

Replace the lower filler piece.
Insert the filler piece pins with their heads toward the top and replace the cotter pins. If the gun is to be used in an E-11 adapter, the filler piece should stick out to the right. Otherwise it can stick out on either side.

Replace the latch, latch spring and latch pin.
Make sure the spring is seated in the holes in the latch and the lower filler piece. Press down on the latch while inserting the pin.

Put back the latch lock
and insert its pin and cotter pin.

Replace the trigger. Put it through its hole, with the long handle part to the rear and the hole for the trigger spring on top. Seat the trigger spring in the hole on the trigger and push the top of the spring back into the hole in the back plate. Put the spacer to the left of the trigger (as seen from behind the gun) and push the trigger pin into place.

Replace the buffer plate and buffer disks.
Put the buffer plate into the buffer tube, small end first, and drop in the disks a few at a time...
. . . Or, if you are working at a steady table, stack up the disks like poker chips, put the buffer plate on top with the small end up, and push the buffer tube down over the stack.

Replace the buffer adjusting screw.
Put the plunger and plunger spring into the hole in the buffer adjusting screw. Tighten the screw until the plunger hits the buffer tube, then hold the plunger down with the tip of a tool and continue to turn the screw until the plunger is held in place.

Adjust the buffer adjusting screw.
When the screw has been tightened as tight as possible—use the caliber .50 combination wrench if one is available—you should not be able to see more than one thread. If it does not go in that far, you have inserted too many buffer disks, or the disks and the buffer plate are not seated correctly. If the screw goes in so far that the end goes inside the buffer tube, the disks are too worn to be used. Have the ordnance shop make the necessary replacements.

No farther in than this.

At least this far in.

Image 6.17
Inside pages, *This is Your Gun* manual.

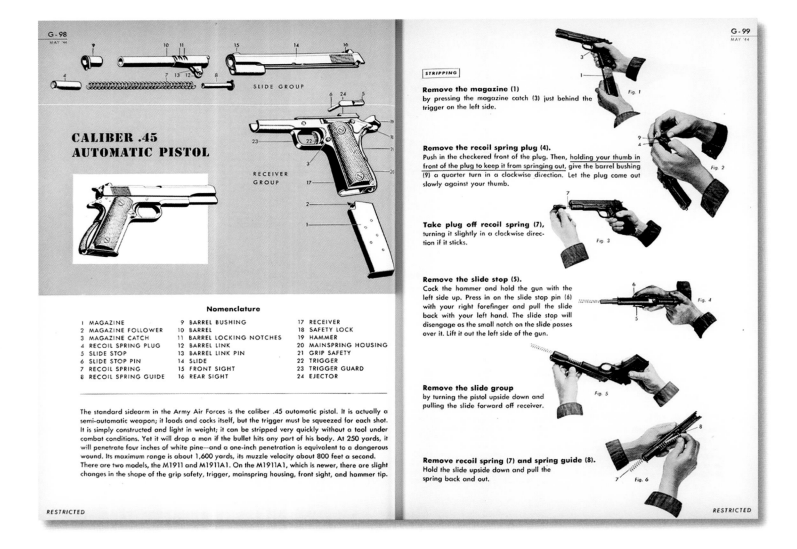

Image 6.18
Inside pages, *This is Your Gun* manual. Illustration indicating profiles of Japanese and German fighter airplanes.

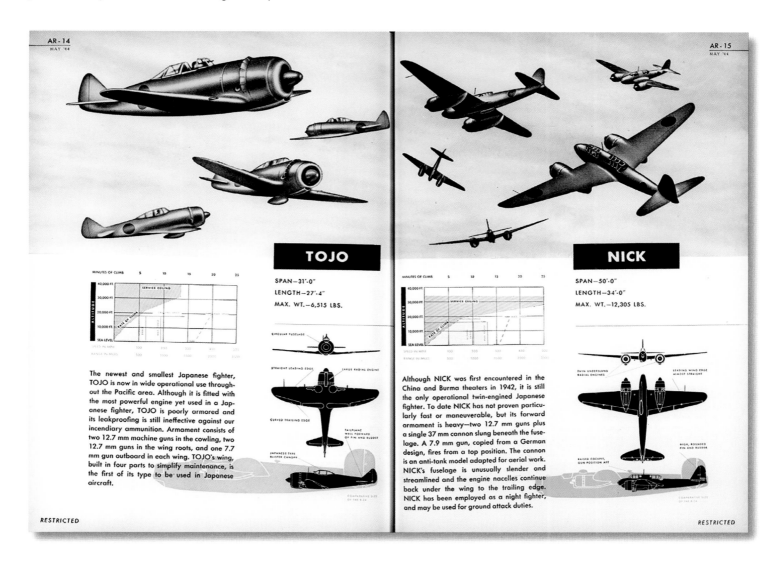

NOTES

1 Will Burtin, "Reflections on Graphic Design" (unpublished manuscript, 1966), 17, Will Burtin Papers, 93.5, Cary Graphic Design Archive, Rochester Institute of Tecchnology.

2 Burtin to Caroll E. Casey, Eastman Kodak Company, July 24, 1962, Will Burtin Papers, 6.2, Cary Graphic Design Archive, RIT.

3 Ellen Lupton, ed., *Beautiful Users: Designing for People* (New York: Princeton Architectural Press, 2014), 21.

4 Cara McCarthy in Lupton, *Beautiful Users*, 26.

5 Sheila Pontis, *Making Sense of Field Research: A Practical Guide for Information Designers* (Oxfordshire, UK: Routledge, 2018), 7.

6 Pontis and Michael Babwahsingh, "Start with the Basics: Understanding Before Doing" (symposium paper, *IIID Vision Plus 2015*, Birmingham City University, UK, September 4, 2015), 90–102, https://www.iiid.net/downloads/IIID-VisionPlus-2015-Proceedings.pdf.

7 "Information Design: Core Competencies— What Information Designers Know and Can Do," Information Design Exchange (idX), Austria: IIID Public Library, August 31, 2007, http://www.iiid.net/PublicLibrary/idx-Core-Competencies-What-information-designers-know-and-can-do.pdf; Kim Baer, *Information Design Workbook: Graphic Approaches, Solutions, and Inspiration + 30 Case Studies* (Beverly, MA: Rockport, 2008).

8 Burtin, "Reflections."

9 Burtin to Dr. Macleod, January 9, 1944, Will Burtin Papers, 98.1, Cary Graphic Design Archive, RIT.

10 *Position Firing Against Fighters Attacking on the Curve of Pursuit*, US Army Air Forces Manual 20 (Washington, DC: Office of Strategic Services, May 1944), 108, Will Burtin Papers, 64.2, Cary Graphic Design Archive, RIT.

11 Burtin, and Laurence P. Lessing, "Interrelations," GRAPHIS 22, vol. 4 (1948): 1.

12 Ibid., 2.

13 Ibid., 2.

14 Ibid.

15 Ibid., 3.

16 General Henry H. Arnold, "Introduction" in *This is Your Gun* (Washington, DC: Office of Strategic Services, 1944), 1.

17 Burtin and Lessing, "Interrelations," 3.

18 Ibid., 1.

19 Ibid.

20 Ibid.

21 Ibid.

6.3
Process Box 3
Case Study 3: *Gunner's Information File* Project (1944)

Conceptual Design

Understanding and Framing the Problem
The US Army Air Force needed to train American recruits as aerial gunners. "The aerial gunner had to be taught a method for measuring off gun deflections against a fighter plane attacking his own bomber, in which the gunner had to judge the correct angle of the fighter's attack, its duration, and allow for the fighter's motion and the speed of his own bomber. ... Each gunner had to learn his gun's mechanism inside out in the shortest possible time."[17]

Target Audience
Young American recruits.

Understanding Content
To gain the necessary knowledge for designing each manual, Burtin studied aerodynamics, took flight training lessons, and learned how to use the guns he needed to explain. This helped him become familiar with the relevant terminologies and activities that trainees would face, and to identify which aspects of the process needed to be included in the manual. In addition, he examined other flight training manuals. The understanding he gained helped him make sense of and explain the complexity involved in this topic in a clear and simple manner.

Idea/Solution
Burtin's initial idea was to create a movie to help new recruits learn how to use the relevant gun, "but tests proved that movies had poor memory value in terms of detail, even upon repeated showings."[18] Therefore, he decided to keep cinematic techniques, like the use of frames, but create a loose-leaf manual instead.

Draft Proposal
To be able to clearly convey the interdependent set of variables involved, Burtin synthesized and decomposed the story (i.e., how to use guns), first introducing the bigger picture of the situation, and then progressively zooming in to show the gunner the relevant measurements he would need to know.

Prototype Design

Visual Translation
Each manual provided step-by-step instructions to assemble and disassemble the gun, and "was broken down into page sequences and each page composed so that pictures and text became part of an accentuated, almost cinematic flow."[19] To remove unnecessarily details, "photographs were silhouetted so as to bring out detail and interpose no square halftone blocks in the visual stream."[20] Other design decisions involved pulling titles out of the text boxes and using typographic style, like bolding, to create a visual hierarchy and facilitate the distinction of different parts of the content, making it more accessible. Title sizes, however, were not set larger "than the body type to avoid disrupting in the sequence of operations."[21]

Image 7.1
Detail of *The Cell* exhibition for the Upjohn Company,
showing the nucleus of the cell, San Francisco, 1958.

Approach

7.1
A Cooperative Way of Working

In this chapter, we examine the fourth dimension–approach–to better understand how to make sense of and effectively design information. Information designers today frequently deal with problems that require multi-layered analysis, requiring rigorous techniques and expert knowledge and skills to move further in the process. Designers themselves may not have the necessary background knowledge to (1) make sense of specialized content, (2) translate concepts into appropriate visual forms or (3) fully understand every aspect of the problem solely through secondary research. To address these challenges, Burtin believed that "cooperative work" (today known as co-design or cross-disciplinary work) was essential to achieve effective results. He felt that it's "impossible to proceed without the help and advice of scientists" and other professionals who are experts in the project at hand.[1] A collaborative approach is particularly important for information design, since research and interactions with a wide range of professionals may be required to make sense of unclear concepts and situations. Even when the design team is small, with one or two people performing various tasks simultaneously while relying mostly on their own knowledge,[2] working closely with specialists will greatly improve the quality of the final outcome.

Burtin felt that outstanding design work in all fields was the "result of direct contact between the decision-maker in a business enterprise and a good designer."[3] In order to obtain a deeper understanding of a subject, he engaged in constant dialogue with professionals from disciplines related to that subject, asking questions, checking his ideas and working together with them. British-based graphic designer F.H.K. Henrion admired Burtin for this approach:

> This activity which is so essential and new that
> Will pioneered, as designer talking to the scientist, ...
> asking questions: 'Could this be shown like this?
> Could it have this color? Could it have this shape?
> Should it be like this? Would this be possible?
> Would this make it clearer?'[4]

Today, collaboration, or "cooperative work," as Burtin called it, is commonplace in many organizations. Designers, clients and other stakeholders in a project tend to work together from the beginning. Burtin alluded to this newly adopted method of working when, in 1966, he described the designer not only as a person creating drawings, but also as a co-planner of the project. To be effective, he maintained, everyone involved in a project – clients, designers, scientists, etc. – needed to work as a unified team. Without becoming experts in each other's domains, they had to share the same information, be aware of technical possibilities and limitations and possess a general sense of the overall plan. Burtin further pointed out that scientists' unfamiliarity with the designer's approach, tools and techniques "is a factor that must be explored carefully by designers and made understandable through cooperative work."[5] This point is even more appropriate now that designers and scientists often work together. During the development of one of his projects, Burtin recalled:

> It came often as a surprise to cooperating scientists that the complex information, which they supplied, resulted in simple dimensional presentations of a type of beauty that enhanced understanding of processes and structural-organic relationships without distorting their significance. However, in designing these structures it was just as surprising and gratifying to realize that the merging of a problem and its most suitable, most economic, interpretation resulted invariably and inevitably in a novel form of strong esthetic impact.[6]

The Cell exhibition described in the next section clearly demonstrates the benefits of working collaboratively with a cross-disciplinary approach. The success of this exhibition was the result of a group of professionals from several disciplines joining forces to reach a common goal: translating something complex into a more understandable form.

7.2
The Cell Exhibition
Burtin's initial concern was to find a way to make the medical research subject, "What is a cell?" understandable to a general audience. His solution was to create a large-scale model of a cell that the Upjohn Company could present as an exhibition at the 1958 San Francisco meeting of the American Medical Association. The model, titled the *Upjohn Cell*, became the first in a series of three-dimensional interpretive exhibitions that Upjohn sponsored over a period of 13 years. (see chapters 4 and 5.)[7]

The model explained scientific "discoveries made possible by recently developed physical and chemical techniques," particularly in the area of cytology. The electron microscope helped reveal the cell's "inner structure down almost to the molecular level, expanding prior research done using the light microscope."[8]

"Through the design," Burtin explained, "random bits and sectors of information were to be 'pulled together' into a logical relationship to each other and to the demonstration as a whole."[9] For initial planning purposes, input from experts in the field was essential. For the next step – creation of the enlarged scale model – Burtin had to figure out how to represent what normally cannot be observed without specialized equipment, due to the cell's microscopic size. George Klauber, a close associate of Burtin's for many years, explained that during this part of the process, "Every doctor and scientist [who collaborated on the project] had a different interpretation of what a cell structure would look like enlarged one million times," and when it became evident that they were not going to reach a consensus, "Will, with characteristic audacity and insight, made the decisions necessary to complete a working model."[10] As a result, certain shapes and individual parts of the cell were depicted abstractly, to produce an optical experience and thereby help viewers understand the cell's interrelated functions.

Image 7.3
Will Burtin standing in front of the completed model
for *The Cell* exhibition, at San Francisco meeting of
the American Medical Association, 1958.

Burtin and his team magnified the basic human cell more than one million times, making a three-dimensional walk-through model in transparent plastic.[11] This physical depiction of the fundamental unit of all life was 24 feet across and 12 feet high. Visitors entered into the three-dimensional maze and interacted with its structure, walking around a labyrinth of plastic tubes and lights. Excluding the cytoplasmic matrix, the various smaller plastic elements of the model depicted all the essential parts of a human cell in correct scale: the nucleolus, nucleus, nuclear membrane, cytoplasm and cell membrane. Pieces of plastic symbolizing mitochondria were scattered throughout, and smaller spheres next to each mitochondrion represented globules of fat. Visitors could see, with the naked eye, all the important structures in a cell.

Burtin described *The Cell* exhibition as presenting:

> A generalized view of an average cell before it develops specialized features that would change it into a muscle cell, a blood cell, a brain cell or an insulin cell. The structure was designed to demonstrate scale and functional relationships between active cell parts–the organelles–and the supporting parts–such as cytoplasm and membrane.[12]

The Cell exhibition was a highlight of Burtin's professional career. Klauber described it as: "An overwhelming success–although a few of the very men who could never take a stand or commit themselves were quick to challenge it."[13] Burtin thought that the key for the exhibition success was that the model:

> accomplished at a glance what the combination of existing means of information had failed to do: it produced an immediate appreciation of a cell's logical structure and functioning. To this one had to add the visual attraction which resulted from the qualities of forms, material, lights and colors; all integrated toward a clear understanding of the whole.[14]

The exhibition helped the general public gain a solid understanding of a basic but complex medical subject and contributed to scientific research by helping professionals shorten their initial study of the cell from months to minutes. As a result, the exhibition generated a great deal of positive attention in both the professional and public press. A major article in *Industrial Design* magazine stated that the model imagined with great graphic inventiveness the plastic shapes and forms that evoke a surrealist world, thus becoming an "educational tool for physicians, cytologists, and students to help visualize more clearly the lower processes of life. ... Burtin found in Surrealism a kind of unconscious or prescient visualization of some of the elements he needed for constructing the cell."[15]

Burtin explained that his work for *The Cell* was to interpret and translate into visual forms what he was reading in books and articles, as well as what scientists were saying. This gave the exhibition an educational value relevant to the general public as well as to students, biologists, biochemists and educators from around the globe. Even though not all visitors agreed with the aesthetics of how certain concepts were represented in the model, its informational value was universally regarded as an excellent contribution to the study of science.[16]

In 1960, Burtin designed a detailed and technical brochure of *The Cell* exhibition that combined images from the original large-scale model with its subsequent smaller version. *The Cell* brochure gave a scientific explanation about each aspect of the human cell that had been enlarged and reproduced in the 24-foot model. The rectangular brochure (8.5 × 5.4 in.) included diagrams throughout to help readers better understand the key scientific concepts illustrated with photographs. (see images 7.7 to 7.13.)

Image 7.4
Fabricator from The Displayers Inc. constructing
The Cell exhibition, 1957.

Image 7.5
The Cell exhibition, in construction, 1957.

Image 7.6
The Cell exhibition, in construction, 1957.

Image 7.7
Cover, *The Cell* brochure, 1960.

Image 7.8
Back cover, *The Cell* brochure, 1960.

Image 7.9
Inside pages, *The Cell* brochure.

Image 7.10
Inside pages, *The Cell* brochure.

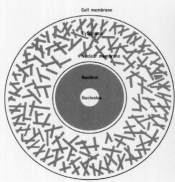

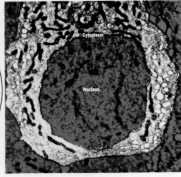

so complicated this is rather difficult, because one must examine many sections and carry in one's mind what has been seen in each, and from these images imagine what the three-dimensional structure is like. This is what the Upjohn giant C.E.L.L. model has done for the viewer—it makes it possible for him to see in three-dimensions all the important structures in a cell with the naked eye. For example, on Page 7 there is an electron micrograph of a cell from a guinea pig pancreas that secretes digestive juice. It shows some mitochondria—the potato-shaped structures—and a drawing of a thin section through one of these structures. Page 6 shows the three-dimensional model constructed by summing up many such slices. On the same basis, all of the parts of the CELL were constructed. With the exception of the cytoplasmic matrix, all parts are represented in correct scale in relation to the size of the CELL. The model does not represent any particular cell, but contains all the structures that every cell must have to carry on its normal functions.

Because it most nearly resembles protoplasm, transparent plastic was used to construct the model. While at first glance it looks like some fantastic modern sculpture, it is actually a factual representation of cell structure somewhat idealized and tastefully rendered. It is an example that truth, honestly rendered, is beautiful.

2

the anatomy of the cell

There are two main parts to a cell, the cytoplasm and the nucleus. The cytoplasm contains the machinery by which the worn-out cellular parts are replaced and food is converted into energy or stored. The nucleus carries the heredity of the organism and also has regulating influence on the whole cell. In the adjacent electron micrograph of a male germ cell of a snail, the gray area is the cytoplasm and the central red area is the nucleus.

THE CELL MEMBRANE: The cell should be conceived of as being entirely enclosed by a thin "skin" or membrane that is ordinarily not visible with light microscopes. By electron microscopy the cell membrane is seen as a mere line of demarcation without definite structure (Page 5). Painstaking physical and chemical methods have failed to elucidate the structure of the cell membrane, but it is believed to be an infinitesimally thin meshwork of fine, elongated protein molecules enmeshing fatty material. It has many deep and complicated outpouchings and infoldings. The outpouchings of adjacent cells interlock to hold them firmly together and thus contribute significantly to the tensile strength of the tissues they form. The CELL model displays a small square segment of the cell membrane (Page 4). The outer surface

3

Images 7.11 to 7.13
Inside pages, *The Cell* brochure.

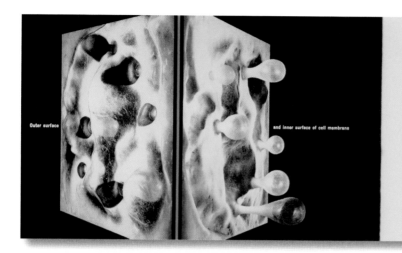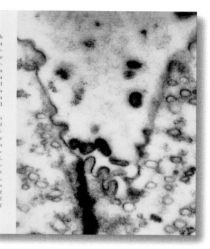

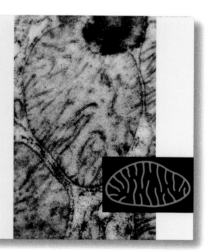

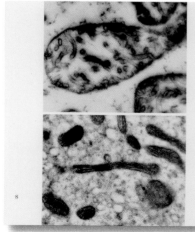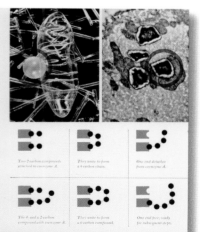

NOTES

1   Will Burtin, "Man is Responsible For His Environment,
    project development," 1971 (for exhibition at the
    United Nations Conference on the Human Environment,
    Stockholm, June 1972), 3, Will Burtin Papers, 9.9–9.10,
    Cary Graphic Design Archive,
    Rochester Institute of Technology.

2   Sheila Pontis, "Guidelines for Conceptual Design to Assist
    Diagram Creators in Information Design Practice" (PhD diss.,
    University of the Arts London, 2012).

3   Burtin, "Untitled Notes" (unpublished, n.d.), 1,
    Will Burtin Papers, 64, Cary Graphic Design Archive, RIT.

4   F.H.K. Henrion, "A Tribute to Will Burtin,"
    Typographic 1 (1972): 2.

5   Burtin, "Reflections on Graphic Design"
    (unpublished manuscript, 1966), 9, Will Burtin Papers, 93.5,
    Cary Graphic Design Archive, RIT.

6   Ibid., 10.

7   *The Cell: An Exhibit Presenting the Basic Unit of Life*
    (Kalamazoo, MI: Upjohn, circa 1958–1960), Will Burtin Papers,
    68.1 and Drawer 55.5–55.6, Cary Graphic Design Archive, RIT.

8   *The Cell: A Scope Monograph on Cytology*
    (Kalamazoo, MI: Upjohn, 1958), 1, Will Burtin Papers, 68.2–68.3,
    Cary Graphic Design Archive, RIT.

9   Burtin, "Reflections," 11.

10 George Klauber, "Remembering Will Burtin,"
    Print (May 1972): 79.

11 Burtin, "Reflections," 12.

12 Ibid.

13 Klauber, "Remembering," 79.

14 Burtin, "Reflections," 12.

15 D.G. Meldrum, ed., "The Design of the Cell," *Industrial Design* 5,
    no. 8 (August 1958): 56.

16 Burtin, "Reflections."

17 Ibid., 12.

18 Ibid., 2.

19 Ibid., 12.

7.3
Process Box 4
Case Study 4: *The Cell* Exhibition (1958)

Conceptual Design

Understanding and Framing the Problem
During the 1950s, significant breakthroughs among drug manufacturing companies occurred. For instance, Upjohn chemists developed new healing medicines to restore basic body functions. New knowledge and scientific discoveries demanded the creation of clear ways of communication that were also different from those of other companies. The communication of that new knowledge to expert and general audiences was the goal of this project.

Target Audience
Scientists, students, and the general public.

Understanding Content
Initially, Burtin focused on collecting information. During this initial research stage, he and his team gathered information by:

- visiting US and European universities and research foundations
- studying the medical literature
- conducting interviews with physicians, biologists, molecular chemists, geneticists and experts in cytology
- studying films and illustrative techniques already created to explain new scientific findings on the human cell
- studying new electron-micrographic observations that had been made at various US research institutions.

Idea/Solution
The team's research clearly indicated that a comprehensive cell model would be useful both for medical practitioners and for high school, university and medical students. Because he realized that the identified scientists had little time for daily reading, Burtin decided that a walk-in model in the form of a three-dimensional cell structure could best portray the data he needed to communicate. This huge cell model unraveled and revealed the inner workings of the microscopic living organism it represented.

The audience had direct, physical access to it, and could experience and absorb firsthand the scientific processes, connections, textures and components involved.

Team Approach
Dr. Garrard Macleod, an Upjohn scientist and Director of Special Projects, coordinated all scientific aspects of the project, and Burtin's studio staff worked on drawings and models alongside the craftsmen who built the full-size structure. "The wealth of documentation and the steady flow of information from participating scientists," Burtin said, "not only made the direction of the design effort clear but also gave assurance that we could count on a successful outcome of the project."[17]

"Gradually, thanks to the generously shared knowledge and adventurous enthusiasm of scientists at the Rockefeller Institute, [Burtin] began building an image in [his] mind, which grew into a structure that fused and united all aspects of the cell. Studies had taken over six months and it took three more months before a first accurate scale model was presented to Upjohn management."[18]

Draft Proposals
Burtin and his team made 150 working drawings of three complete scale models and about 20 sketch models of parts.

Prototype Design

Visual Translation
"After building a first small-scale model, a critical review by scientists of all its parts took place, until the specialized functions of cell division, heredity, molecular chemistry and energy storage had also been considered and integrated. After this, the building of a large and final model could be undertaken."[19] Burtin compared notes with the experts and cross-referenced draft versions of the model with their recommendations. However, on more than one occasion, the scientists did not agree about the shapes and forms to use for the model. Ultimately, Burtin had to depend on what his research had taught him to make final decisions.

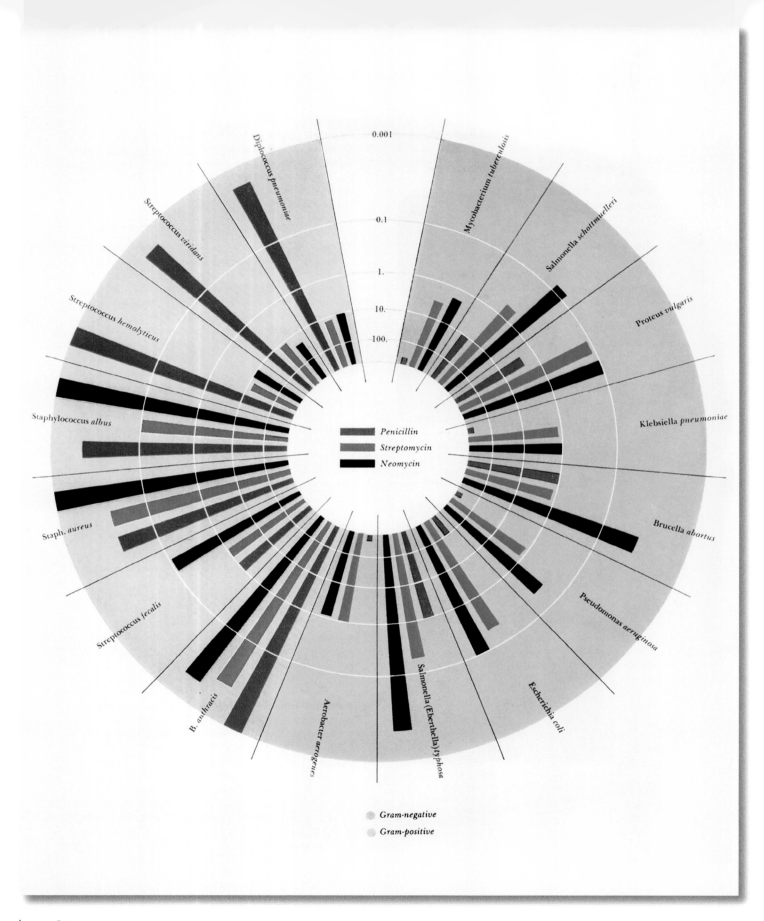

Image 8.1
Diagram from *SCOPE* magazine on the effectiveness
of antibiotics: penicillin (blue), streptomycin (red)
and neomycin (black), 1951.

Outcome

8.1

Integration of Content

We have seen how Burtin's scientific approach to design, in his exhibition work especially, achieved a conceptual and visual balance that helped his audience understand the scientific content he was trying to convey. This chapter examines the harmony between function/form and understanding that typifies effective design. Burtin described this relationship as "integration":

> In my designs I aim at integration. I feel that, as design factors, form and color can be controlled at least as much as aspects of texture and time. In other words, I attempt to provide a visual structure that expresses the thoughts and feelings inherent in the problem at hand in a coherent way in order to achieve easy understanding and immediate impact.[1]

By experimenting with various materials such as transparent plastics, steel, aluminum and lightweight new materials, Burtin integrated his content and presentation into a cohesive whole.[2] In the work he produced for brochures, manuals, magazines and other print formats, he combined a modernist visual quality with a functional style. His font choices were mostly sans serifs; he used contrast and white space in his designs; he favored asymmetric layouts with large margins to integrate color, photographs, sketches, illustrations and other graphic elements; and he loved basic geometric forms and primary colors.

In information design, the unification of form, color, texture and content effectively leads to deeper understanding only when these components are part of a well-thought-out rationale. Putting the proper elements together harmoniously can bring about this unity, but requires logical thought. Richard Saul Wurman emphasizes that style must not become "the engine" of the train of design, but remain simply "a passenger."[3] Similarly, Burtin, many years earlier, stressed that "Beauty is not necessarily a matter of form or style, but a result of order achieved," and that "The finest and highest order is the one which results in such simplicity of statement that it could not be said more constructively, more encompassing, more spirited. *That* is beauty. *That* has human dignity."[4] A message is communicated effectively when this type of beauty is achieved and the audience gains a better understanding of the information through "visual reasoning."[5]

According to Robert McKim, visual reasoning is the process of changing or expanding the understanding of a concept, phenomenon or object by looking at information presented in visual form.[6] Graphics, diagrams, models and other visual forms can extend human vision and present a new reality. Integrating content, function and form is essential to achieving both a highly informative and understandable design. Burtin similarly felt that for visual reasoning to succeed, the designer should employ "any and every means" to achieve integration and clarity, regardless of the visual techniques used (photography, painting, movies, drawings, 3D exhibitions, etc.).[7] Burtin's work on *Fortune* and *SCOPE* magazines, discussed in the next section, will demonstrate the range of visual techniques he used to effectively enable visual reasoning and how he mastered the integration of function, form and understanding to produce effective information design outcomes.

8.2
Fortune and *SCOPE* Magazines

Burtin was art director of *Fortune* magazine from 1946 to 1949. *Fortune* had been founded in 1930 by Henry Robinson Luce (also founder of *TIME* magazine) to "nothing less than explain the way the world worked," but to explain it differently than the other business periodicals of the day. "*Fortune* stories took many forms: personality profiles, dynastic sagas and chronicles of scientific advances" as well as stories about successful or interesting businesses, all of which gave the magazine its unique style.[8] To ensure that it would remain fresh and modern, *Fortune* always employed young writers. Accomplished photographers and illustrators joined with them to produce an engaging product, in contrast to the other magazines of that time, that mostly reported abstract stories with complex graphs.

Burtin's main contributions to *Fortune* as its art director were revamping the magazine's organizational structure and initiating its modernist tone and personality. He transformed the role of the magazine's art director from that of a "layout man" to one involved in management and content development along with the editorial staff. Thus, Burtin moved from the drawing board to the boardroom, until he was on a par with *Fortune*'s managerial policy makers. This was a major development in the history of design. Burtin also gave *Fortune* a different look, establishing what he would later call his "new discipline on design." Ladislav Sutnar described Burtin's new way of designing as using "new visual techniques for maps, graphs and charts."[9] The visualization of complexity, he wrote, was based on a two-step process: "First, of extracting from a complex subject the irreducible essentials; and second, of exposing these essentials in the light of controlled design in a way to make them self-explanatory."[10] In short, Burtin integrated typography and imagery with content, in order to communicate more clearly.

To ensure high standards of visualization, Burtin hired designers and graphic artists who possessed the greatest talent and mastery. He sought out artists with the most appropriate sets of skills to visually communicate the topics in each edition. As art director, Burtin left the execution of his ideas to others but remained in charge of the strategy behind that execution. His challenge at *Fortune* was to externalize his thinking and clearly articulate his vision and ideas to others. He was superbly able to accomplish this task because his vision was so strong; he was also able to commission the work to some of the best available creative individuals of his time. In supervising the commissioned artwork, he made sure that the message was being communicated with clarity and, at the same time, that it was in line with the overall visual appearance he wanted for the magazine.

SCOPE

As a result, *Fortune*'s "*Burtin* era" became a showcase of the finest talent of the period. The magazine covers were always a priority, since they created the first impression. To create the covers, Burtin brought in American modernist designers such as Lester Beall, E. McKnight Kauffer, Matthew Leibowitz, Alvin Lustig and Herbert Matter. Popular artists of the time such as Hananiah Harai, Edmund Lewandowski and Walter Tandy Murch contributed covers as well. For the interior pages, he commissioned work to such renowned designers and graphic artists as Max Gschwind, Alex Steinweiss and Ladislav Sutnar. Burtin favored fellow European immigrant designers such as Herbert Bayer and George Giusti; fine art paintings by Dong Kingman, Jacob Lawrence, Hans Moller and Ben Shahn; and photography by Ansel Adams, Walker Evans and Ezra Stoller also appeared in the pages of *Fortune*. This consistent use of a broad selection of highly creative professionals, selectively matched with appropriate content, gave *Fortune* a vitality that made the magazine stand out.

Burtin left *Fortune* in 1949 to start his own design studio. The Upjohn Pharmaceutical Company soon became his principal client. Upjohn hired Burtin to art direct its occasional biomedical journal, *SCOPE*, targeted at doctors, pharmacists and other health professionals. Burtin had designed *SCOPE*'s premier issue in 1941 and then turned the publication's reins over to his peer, American designer Lester Beall. Beall continued to design *SCOPE* throughout the 1940s, until Burtin returned as its art director in late 1949 and stayed on until its last issue in 1957.

When Burtin started working on *SCOPE* magazine, medicine was advancing rapidly. Many common medications at that time had not been available 20 or even 10 years earlier. The rapid increase of new drugs being brought to market generated a new demand: physicians had to be kept informed about these advances. The magazine's challenge was to explain the latest medical research, report on advances in diagnoses and treatments, and educate physicians about Upjohn's new prescription drugs in order to create demand for them. Burtin admitted that *SCOPE* had a "complicated nature," requiring more attention and study from physicians than the other, more conventional pharmaceutical company house organs required of them, because of its scholarly nature:

It [was] necessary to supplement the efforts of the sales representative with various forms of literature. These fall into two categories-the first, which is brief and eye-catching and aims merely to remind the doctor that you have available a product whose purpose and use he already knows-and the other, which is less arresting but much longer and is designed to acquaint the doctor with products that he either does not know at all or is only partially familiar with. This latter form of literature, while necessary to the successful promotion of a product, partakes in character much more of the scientific paper than of advertising in the ordinary sense. For this reason, it is often published in forms suitable to its content-scientific monographs and scientific journals. These latter are the house organs, which a number of the leaders in the industry have put out.[11]

For *SCOPE* to differentiate itself from other similar, successful pharmaceutical company house organs of the time, it needed a distinctive format and character of its own. The result was a large format (11.25 × 9 in.) and highly visual magazine including discussions of Upjohn products, featuring one product in each issue, and reviews of medical subjects. Articles that were not strictly about medicine, but which might be relevant and of interest to physicians, were also added as a "Science and Culture" section.[12]

So it could be said that *SCOPE* was a scientific journal in the form of an educational magazine, meant to explain to doctors and others the development of new drugs, their purposes, and how to use them. *SCOPE*'s uniqueness among the specialized magazines of its genre was based on its rich technical content, the innovative ways in which Burtin visually explained that content, and the range of different textures he used for the magazine's pages themselves. Burtin felt that the 'tactile' factor was essential to emphasize the believability of the text, because doctors use their hands in the practice of medicine.[13] Feeling the content would increase its credibility.

SCOPE's visual and diagrammatic approach to scientific content allowed the magazine to clearly articulate complicated topics, reduce complexity and create "a certain beauty of clear statement."[14] The power of its graphic symbolism is, perhaps, most clearly displayed in its covers during the 16 years it was published. *SCOPE* remains to this day a benchmark of the effective integration of form and content.

Cover, SCOPE Magazine, Volume 1, Issue 1, 1941

The Upjohn Company selected Burtin to create the cover for the first issue of SCOPE magazine in 1941. Against a metallic silver background, he used a layering approach, integrating a number of symbolic elements: a test tube, a baby, a hand, a leaf and a flower. The black-and-white photograph of his hand holding a test tube is combined with composite images of a baby atop a leaf, seeking a butterfly, a direct reference to a detail in the classic da Vinci painting, *The Virgin of the Rocks*. The implied message here is the idea of a "test-tube baby," which could be seen as predicting in-vitro fertilization, introduced in 1978.

Burtin chose the elegant Didot Bodoni typeface for the SCOPE masthead. The rhetorical nature of the cover provides a glimpse into Burtin's process of designing. At the time, this cover (see image 8.2) was notable because of its visionary indirect messaging and its effective use of symbolism.

Diagram from SCOPE Magazine on Antibiotics, 1951

One of Burtin's classic diagrams appeared in the Fall 1951 issue of SCOPE magazine. This diagram compares the impact of three antibiotic drugs on bacterial skin infections: penicillin (blue), streptomycin (red) and neomycin (black). The radial structure of the diagram organizes these antibiotics around the central point in red, blue and black bands as they are used to combat the various infections. (see image 8.1.) Gram positive infections are grouped in the light red section of the diagram, and gram negative infections in the light blue. The effectiveness of the antibiotics is expressed as the highest dilution in ɥ/ml which inhibits the test organism. Higher dilutions move towards the periphery; consequently, the length of the colored bar is proportional to the effectiveness. (For example, the diagram shows that penicillin is most effective against gram positive infections.)

Diagram from SCOPE Magazine on the Brain, 1955

The winter 1955 issue of SCOPE magazine featured a cover and major article on the physiology and pharmacology of emotion. The diagram shown on the table of contents page identifies the 23 major parts of the brain. (see image 8.6.)

Cover, SCOPE Magazine on Blood Pressure, 1954

Central Control of Blood Pressure was the feature article in the SCOPE issue that highlighted one of Burtin's most iconic and successful covers. The cover is a white and gray, full-page diagram of the brain's role in the human central nervous system. (see image 8.5.) It shows the thalamus opticus, nucleus lentiformis, cerebellum, cortex cerebri and other key structures of the brain that are involved in the control of blood pressure. Nerves are color-coded according to their function. This visual provided a compelling opening for the issue's major theme article.

Diagram from SCOPE Magazine on the GI Tract, 1954

In this issue, SCOPE featured an article titled *Innervation of the Gastrointestinal Tract*. The larger diagram depicts the innervation of the gastrointestinal tract. Functional relationships of the reciprocal innervation are stressed rather than shown as a realistic representation of anatomy. The photographic face and the silhouette brain indicate that responses to life situations profoundly influence gastrointestinal function through autonomic nerve supply. The color of each dot in which a nerve ends indicates its effect: stimulation (green) or inhibition (red).

The smaller diagram on the bottom right shows a longitudinal section of the intestine and indicates the innervation, including the afferent nerve fibers of the various muscle layers and the mucosa. Both diagrams show sympathetic fibers (blue lines), parasympathetic fibers (yellow lines) and afferent fibers (black lines). The myriad levels of scientific information presented in these diagrams are effective in their symbolic simplicity. (see image 8.7.)

Cover and Article, SCOPE Magazine on the Brain, 1957

This SCOPE issue from 1957 included articles on thinking and the brain, topics conceptually conveyed on the cover by combining typography, photographic image, graphic elements and diagrams. (see image 8.9.) In this issue, the feature article, *164 years or 1 Hour*, is illustrated with a diagram that uses shapes, type, and color to show key stages of the thought process, which is recreated in a giant electronic "brain." (see image 8.10.)

Image 8.2
Cover, *SCOPE* magazine, Volume 1, Issue 1, 1941.

Image 8.3
Cover, *SCOPE* magazine on graphs, Spring 1953.

Image 8.4
Inside pages, *Telling Lines–Some Notes on Graphs* article,
SCOPE magazine on graphs, Spring 1953.

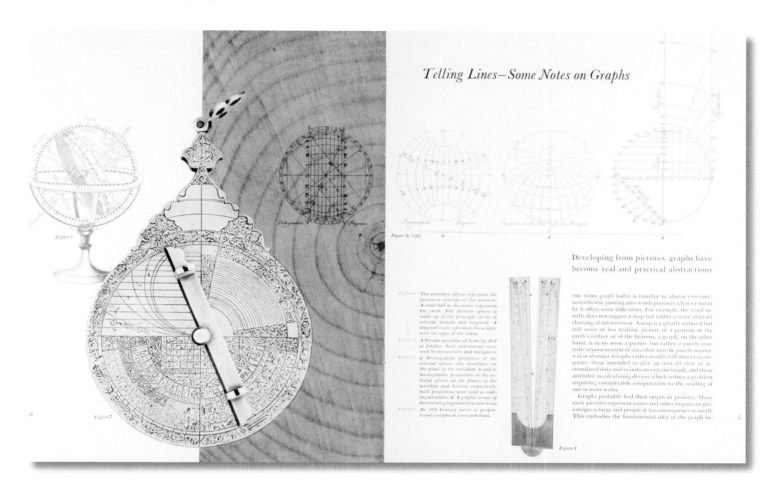

Cover and Article, *SCOPE* Magazine on Graphs, 1953
One of *SCOPE*'s classic covers and its accompanying
article appeared in Spring 1953. The cover combined
graphic elements, including straight black and wavy
pink lines and black circles of various sizes; and
photographic elements, communicating abstract and
more realistic meanings. One of the pink lines divides
the background, creating a strong plane of color on
the right side of the cover.

The first spread of the feature article, titled *Telling
Lines–Some Notes on Graphs*, includes four figures. Figure 1
represents the geocentric concept of the universe, while
Figure 2 is a black-and-white photograph of an instrument
used by astronomers and navigators. Figure 3 is composed of a
sequence of orthographic and stereographic projections; and
the last figure represents a compass in ivory and brass from the
18th century. Together, these four figures provide an overview
of the evolution from pictures to more abstract graphs.

Cover, *SCOPE* Magazine on Heredity, 1957
This cover was one of Burtin's most significant designs for
SCOPE magazine. The cover graphic introduces the issue's
featured article, *The Heredity Material*. A helical set of
progressive dots frames small DNA images, all placed on a
metallic silver background. (see image 8.8.) The helical dot
configuration was later adapted for use on the back cover of
the brochure for Burtin's *Visual Aspects of Science* exhibition.
(see chapter 9.)

Image 8.5
Cover, *SCOPE* magazine on blood pressure, 1954.

Image 8.6

Diagram from *SCOPE* magazine indicating key parts of the brain, 1955.

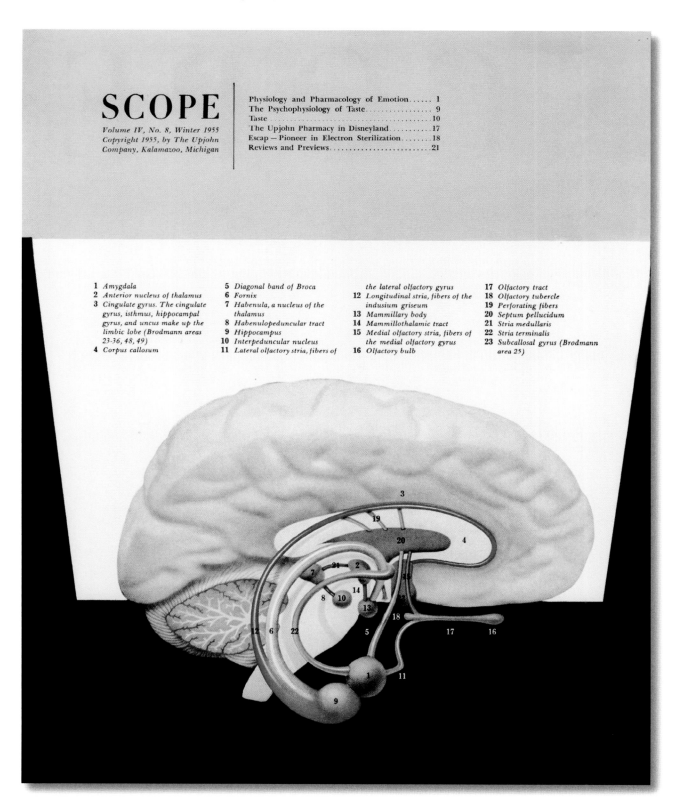

Image 8.7
Diagram from *SCOPE* magazine article on the GI tract, 1954.

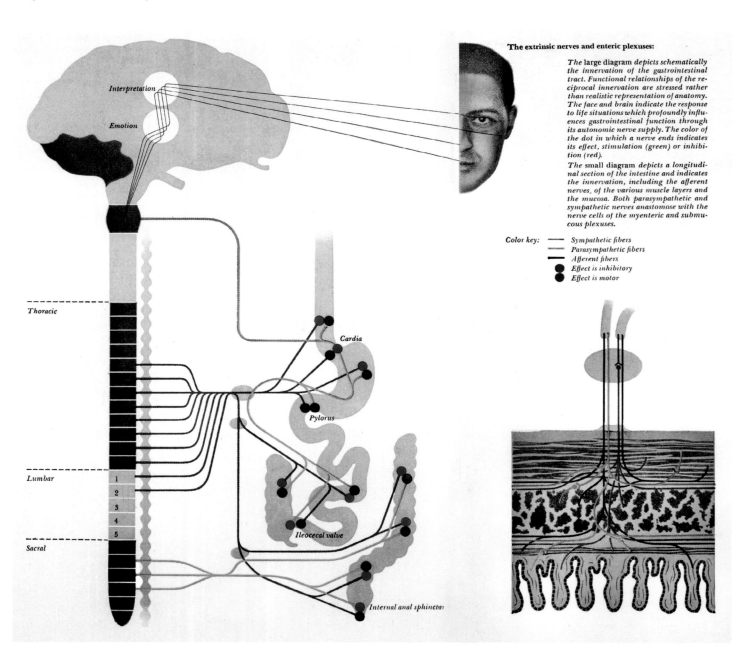

The extrinsic nerves and enteric plexuses:

The large diagram *depicts schematically the innervation of the gastrointestinal tract. Functional relationships of the reciprocal innervation are stressed rather than realistic representation of anatomy. The face and brain indicate the response to life situations which profoundly influences gastrointestinal function through its autonomic nerve supply. The color of the dot in which a nerve ends indicates its effect, stimulation (green) or inhibition (red).*

The small diagram *depicts a longitudinal section of the intestine and indicates the innervation, including the afferent nerves, of the various muscle layers and the mucosa. Both parasympathetic and sympathetic nerves anastomose with the nerve cells of the myenteric and submucous plexuses.*

Color key:
— *Sympathetic fibers*
— *Parasympathetic fibers*
— *Afferent fibers*
● *Effect is inhibitory*
● *Effect is motor*

Image 8.8
Cover, *SCOPE* magazine on heredity, 1957.

Image 8.9
Cover, *SCOPE* magazine on the brain, 1957.

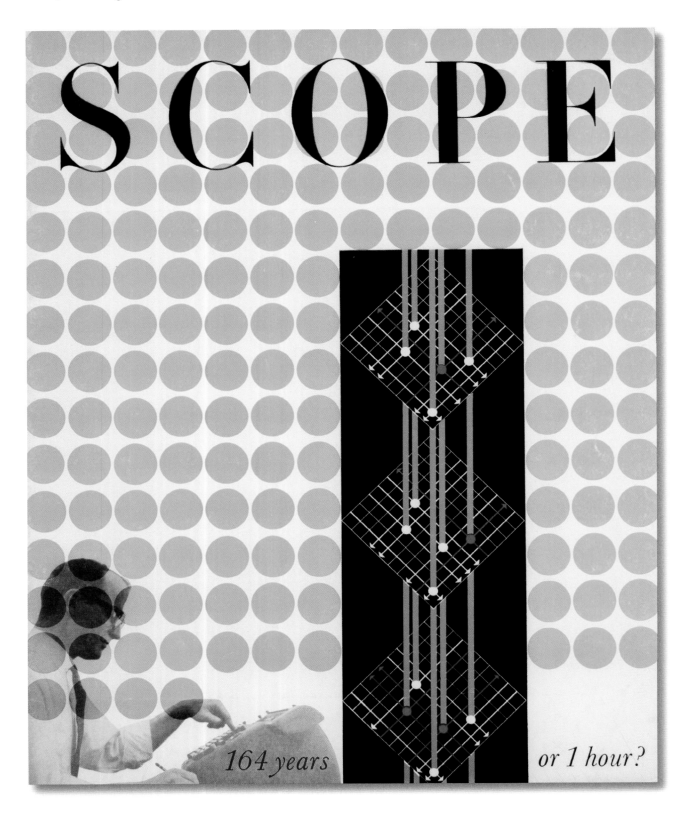

Image 8.10
Inside page, *164 Years or 1 Hour?* article, *SCOPE* magazine on the brain, 1957.

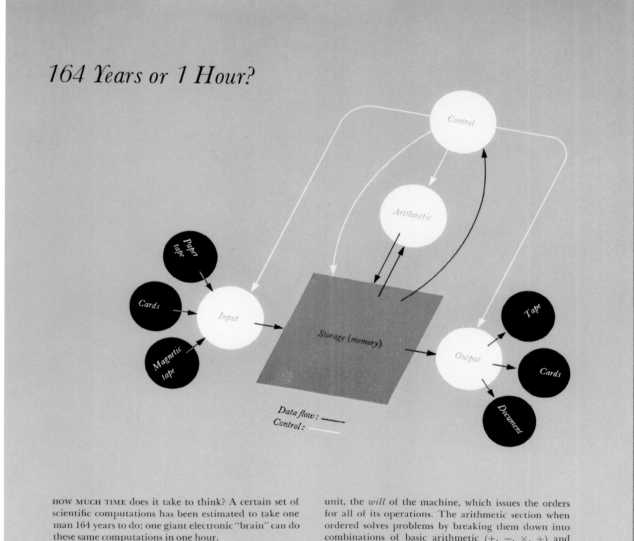

164 Years or 1 Hour?

HOW MUCH TIME does it take to think? A certain set of scientific computations has been estimated to take one man 164 years to do; one giant electronic "brain" can do these same computations in one hour.

The input unit (sensory receptors) in such a machine receives stimuli and translates them into electrical impulses of various sorts. The stimuli may come from magnetic tapes, punched cards, or in the future from the printed page or spoken word. The electronic impulses generated by these stimuli are immediately coded into computer *language* as numbers of seven digits or more, called *words*. These words are transmitted to the *memory* or data storage unit, after being assigned individual addresses. Immense amounts of data can be remembered by the machine for use as directed by the control unit, the *will* of the machine, which issues the orders for all of its operations. The arithmetic section when ordered solves problems by breaking them down into combinations of basic arithmetic ($+$, $-$, $\times$, $\div$) and makes data comparisons or arrangements. The results are then either returned to the memory section or are recorded automatically by the output unit in printed form, on punched cards, or on magnetic tape.

The machine including the control unit is, however, a complete robot which does only what the human mathematician (*programmer*) tells it to do. He, the *deus ex machina*, gives detailed instructions on every operation or calculation to be performed by the computer. These programs may, however, be stored in the memory unit for solving future problems.

11

NOTES

1   Will Burtin, "Notes on Visual Design"
    (unpublished notes, n.d.), 1, Will Burtin Papers, 97.3,
    Cary Graphic Design Archive,
    Rochester Institute of Technology.

2   Philip B. Meggs, *A History of Graphic Design*, 3rd ed.
    (New York: John Wiley, 1998).

3   Richard S. Wurman, "Hats,"
    Design Quarterly 145 (1989): 1–32.

4   Burtin, "A Program in Print: Upjohn and Design"
    Print 9, no. 5 (insert, May/June 1955): 36; also in
    Will Burtin Papers, 77.5, Cary Graphic Design Archive, RIT.

5   Ibid, 36.

6   Robert H. McKim, *Thinking Visually:*
    A Strategy Manual for Problem Solving
    (Belmont, CA: Lifetime Learning, 1980).

7   Burtin and Lawrence P. Lessing, "Interrelations,"
    Graphis 22, vol. 4 (1948), 109.

8   Daniel Okrent, "How the World Really Works,"
    Fortune (September 19, 2005), http://archive.fortune.com/
    magazines/fortune/fortune_archive/
    2005/09/19/8272901/index.htm.

9   Ladislav Sutnar, *Visual Design in Action*, eds.
    Reto Caduff and Steven Heller, 1st ed.
    (New York: Hastings House, 1961); facsimile reprint
    (Zurich: Lars Müller, 2015), Introduction.

10 Ibid.

11 Burtin, "A Program," 44.

12 Ibid., 49.

13 Carol Burtin-Fripp, email message to the author,
    December 2019.

14 Burtin, "A Program," 36

15 Burtin and Lessing, "Interrelations," 5.

16 Burtin, "Reflections on Graphic Design"
    (unpublished manuscript, 1966), 12, Will Burtin Papers, 93.5,
    Cary Graphic Design Archive, RIT.

17 Burtin, "A Program," 50.

18 Burtin, "A Program."

19 Ibid. 49.

20 Ibid, 49-50.

Conceptual Design

Understanding and Framing the Problem

To design a new magazine for the drug manufacturer Upjohn that would "at once link the character of the advertiser with the nature of the pharmaceutical business and its scientific background."[15] The goal was to communicate and educate readers on new pharmaceutical drugs, their purposes and best uses.

Target Audience

Physicians, pharmacists, other health professionals and Upjohn sales representatives.

Understanding Content

"The method is perhaps more cumbersome than most because both author and designer must familiarize themselves with the available material and they must be willing to alter their viewpoints freely."[16]

Idea/Solution

Burtin wanted to design the magazine not as a decorative piece, but to help convey the scientific content it contained. Covers especially were designed to suggest some important aspect of the contents and interior pages were "functional first and decorative incidentally."[17] For each article, copy and design were integrated to make an effective composition in which visuals helped enhance and clarify scientific ideas. The story was analyzed to identify what parts benefitted from the use of visuals such as tables, graphs, photographs and diagrams.[18]

Prototype Design

Visual Translation

Burtin's use of graphic tools and visuals such as typography, diagram, symbol, color and photography was consistently and appropriately integrated with the special requirements of the content. Choosing the format was important both to make the journal stand out and to make it appropriate to physicians. Other existing journals varied greatly in style, from conservative (using design sparingly) to modern (displaying more obvious and even flamboyant design decisions). The former style "seemed inappropriate for a journal devoted to a rapidly progressing science"; a more contemporaneous approach was what *SCOPE* needed.[19] Burtin created highly progressive designs based on strong concepts "couched in an idiom that partook of the scientific in its clarity and definiteness" and where design was an "integral part of the scientific presentations."[20]

Image 9.8 Detail
Diagram from *Will Burtin: Visual Aspects of Science* brochure,
showing nerve pathways of the brain, by which visual (red) and
auditory (green) impulses travel to relay stations–the geniculates–
and to coding centers–the cortices, 1962.

CHAPTER 9

Practice

9.1
Conveying the Value of Information Design

At the end of the 1940s, Burtin pointed out the need for creating clear communications to help people understand the societal, economic and medical changes that were occurring globally. In the 1960s, he suggested that we were entering "the beginning of a new era in communication." The changing environment had demanded "new solutions to problems of learning, of memorizing, of selection and of language specialization."[1] New communication media created a larger spectrum of choice that helped give substance to new means and extend the use of existing media formats. Burtin asserted that comprehensive design could "bring out the clarity, logic and beauty necessary in communication and in all fields where problems of progress are involved."[2] More recently, professor of design Richard Buchanan reported a similar shift among designers. He saw them as moving "toward a new engagement with the problems of everyday experience," since they were developing new products that incorporated knowledge from many different fields of specialized inquiry.[3] Burtin's work had ushered in this shift: more specialized expertise and new skills (not exclusively related to design per se) became essential for developing quality solutions.

Burtin realized that designing for content that is difficult to understand, and involves large amounts of disorganized data, demands more efficient communication techniques. He saw "speeding understanding" as a way to communicate new scientific findings and emerging ideas in an increasingly changing world. Business organizations in different fields were suggesting "that new design approaches to information transmission could be a source of authoritative prestige and give them an image of confidence and purposeful direction."[4] Altogether, these changes demanded "a comprehensive design system … a total design concept that relates the experience range of our communication traditions to a new creativity that is liberated by the new technologies and by still newer ones to be created."[5] Surrounded by this frantically evolving environment, Burtin called for introspective reflection and change within the design community.

As a result, a more holistic way of solving problems emerged among some designers. This new approach meant, first, that designers and content experts would work together as professionals with diverse background knowledge. Next, designers would make decisions based on facts, the audience's needs, and evidence, rather than on their own personal taste. Third, they would adopt a more systematic way of working, moving away from addressing each problem in isolation. Finally, designers would make it a priority to develop an awareness of the complex interrelations between design problems themselves and how they influence design outcomes. In previous chapters, we have shown how Burtin recommended this four-fold approach to solving design problems. Burtin described it as a scientific approach to design, involving research, systems thinking, rigor, and cooperative work. He believed that the designer would be best prepared to adopt these techniques when he became more familiar with the methods of science.[6] Today, information designers are the design professionals who most closely adhere to Burtin's scientific approach to solving design problems.

9.2
Information Design Practice Today

More than 60 years ago, Burtin saw that there was a "great deal of evidence for the conclusion that design products themselves [would] improve their esthetic quality by employing scientific procedures."[7] He wrote that no one had imagined that this approach was also going to "lead to a new and basic social importance of design–far beyond its [then] strong occupation with commercial and sales service functions–into areas in which automation and electronic data processing have so far been incapable of solving conceptual and decision problems."[8]

The practice of information design today has broadened to cope with the diverse challenges of contemporary life, from the design of tangible artifacts (framed challenges) like infographics to the design of less tangible solutions (less framed challenges) that can help viewers understand realities of an environment–like the communication of scientific information and the improvement of dialogue, services and experiences.[9] Echoing Burtin's experience, these current challenges demand a more systematic and rigorous way of working, as teams of professionals from various fields– marketing, design, engineering, technology, social sciences, computer sciences and medical sciences–work together to both generate and execute ideas.

The role of design practitioners has been transformed from being merely creators to being facilitators of dialogue, collaboration and understanding.[10] Increasingly, information designers use their skills to advance communication among team members by sharing ideas and externalizing thinking. Once again, ahead of his time and setting a precedent for this new role, Burtin acted as facilitator in certain instances during the creation of his exhibitions. His "designer's visual training" put him "in a position to see beyond the ideas of [the] science advisers and surprise them with more correct interpretations. This [did] not make [him] a scientist, but it prove[d] that design can be an important vehicle of scientific exploration," and can promote collaboration.[11]

In addition, specialization has become a key requisite. In the 1920s, commercial artists worked as illustrators, letterers and typographic designers.[12] Later, in the 1960s, graphic designers developed a wider repertoire of skills. Currently, information designers typically focus on specific types of projects (often related to enhancing understanding), acting as consultants or art directors, or creating the solutions.

The scientific approach to design, as modeled by Burtin, is a methodology that is becoming more commonplace in practice for today's information designers. And it's changing the way professionals from other disciplines interact with them. Information designers are not only in charge of creating effective functional solutions but are also seen as equal partners in exploring and improving the human condition. These changes in the field demand a new educational approach in order to properly equip future designers, which will be discussed in the next chapter.

9.3
Visual Journeys of Will Burtin's Scientific Approach

Toward the end of his career, Burtin designed two major exhibitions that presented many of his most effective design projects: *Visual Aspects of Science* and *The Communication of Knowledge* exhibitions. His goal was to bring science closer to a general audience and show how design results can be greatly enhanced when a scientific approach to design is embraced. Both exhibitions illustrate the transition from the non-scientific to the scientific era; the evolution of Burtin's journey as a designer; and the development of visualization as a language to communicate the complexity of a range of phenomena.

9.3.1
Visual Aspects of Science Exhibition (1962)

This was a touring retrospective exhibition, created in 1962, showcasing Burtin's work for his major clients: Eastman Kodak Company, International Business Machines (IBM), Upjohn Pharmaceutical Company, and Union Carbide Company. The exhibition, which traveled to Amsterdam, London, Paris and Brussels, focused on several underlying features of science, such as complex models of spacecraft, industrial processes, chemical compounds, metabolic processes in the human body and alternative approaches to medical research.

Novel ideas and discoveries that had been introduced by new scientific and technological developments were presented by alternating scales: the miniature became gigantic and the gigantic minute. This approach invited visitors to experience a journey through "things that are far outside the range of human perception," such as the microscopic, the far distant and the too slow, which often are accessible only through microscopes, telescopes and cameras.[13] In the exhibition space, "microscopic and macroscopic perspectives" could be observed on the walls through a range of "gigantic prints of colorful cell membranes, swirling chromosomes, and hovering uranium atoms." Sitting on pedestals around the space were "minute plastic copies of large scientific models" and in the center, "a colossal, illuminated sculpture of a human brain" was displayed.[14]

In this exhibition, Burtin succeeded in showcasing the principles that today give information design its special character:

1 Simplicity to assist perception (recognition) and recall (memory);
2 Logic in the relationship between content and appearance;
3 Emphasis on the basic idea of the message.[15]

Visitors attending the exhibition were given a red square brochure (9.7 × 9.7 in.) titled *Will Burtin: Visual Aspects of Science*.[16] It presented novel scientific discoveries and new knowledge, using a range of scientific visualizations combining diagrams, drawings and photographs of close-ups and models. (see images 9.1 to 9.9.)

The introduction of the brochure was printed on a translucent vellum sheet atop a black-and-white time-lapse photograph showing lines of light that formed spheres around a white center. Throughout the brochure, various types of papers were used, as well as embossing and various other experimental (at the time) printing techniques. Some pages were even printed on heavily texturized chipboard.

Image 9.1
Cover, *Will Burtin: Visual Aspects of Science* brochure, 1962.

Image 9.2
Back cover, *Will Burtin: Visual Aspects of Science* brochure, 1962.

This is a simplified diagram of a DNA
(desoxyribonucleic acid) molecule, the carrier
of hereditary functions in the cell.

Acknowledgements

*Mr. Roy Tillotson
is Manager of Art, Design and Photography,
Public Relations Department, of the Union
Carbide Corporation, New York City.
Dr. A. Garrard Macleod
is Director of Special Science Projects, The
Upjohn Company, Kalamazoo, Michigan.
Mr. Bruce MacKencie
is Editor of the I.B.M. Journal of Research
and Development, and Director of Scientific
Information, International Business Machines
Corporation, New York City.*

Designed by Will Burtin, New York City

Type setting, reproduction and printing by Fritz Busche, Dortmund, Western Germany

Photographs by Ezra Stoller, Rye, New York

Image 9.3
Inside pages, *Will Burtin: Visual Aspects of Science* brochure.

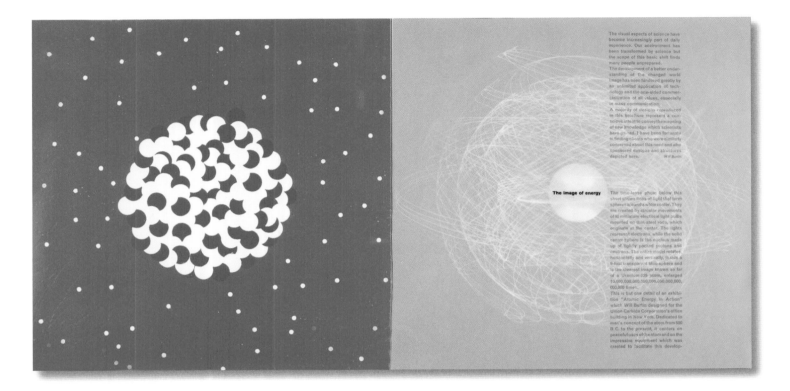

Dramatic images related to Burtin's prior exhibitions and major projects appeared in the brochure: a human blood cell enlarged 250,000 times (a smaller size model built after *The Cell* exhibition); a DNA molecule; the structure of a chromosome; nerve cells of the human brain; and close-up imagery from *The Cell* and *The Brain* exhibitions. The brochure concluded with a photograph of Eastman Kodak Company's *Magic Carpet* World's Fair Building.

The content of the brochure was written by Burtin, Roy Tillotson from Union Carbide Company, Dr. A. Garrard Macleod of Upjohn and Bruce MacKenzie from IBM. Describing it, Burtin wrote, "A majority of designs reproduced in this brochure represent a conscious intent to convey the meaning of new knowledge which scientists have gained. I have been fortunate in finding clients who were similarly concerned about this need and who sponsored the designs and structures depicted here."[17]

Images 9.4 and 9.5
Inside pages, *Will Burtin: Visual Aspects of Science* brochure.

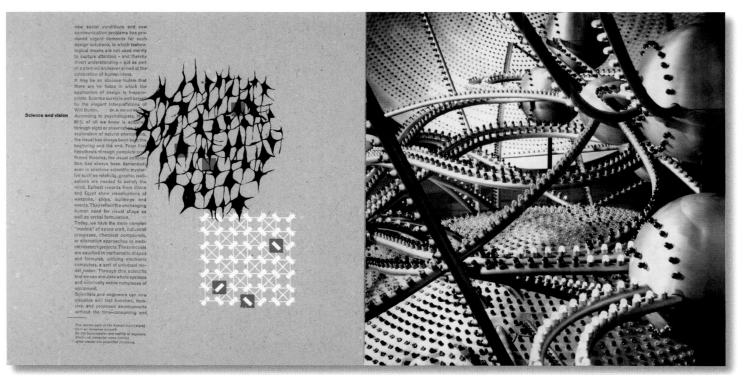

Images 9.6 and 9.7
Inside pages, *Will Burtin: Visual Aspects of Science* brochure.

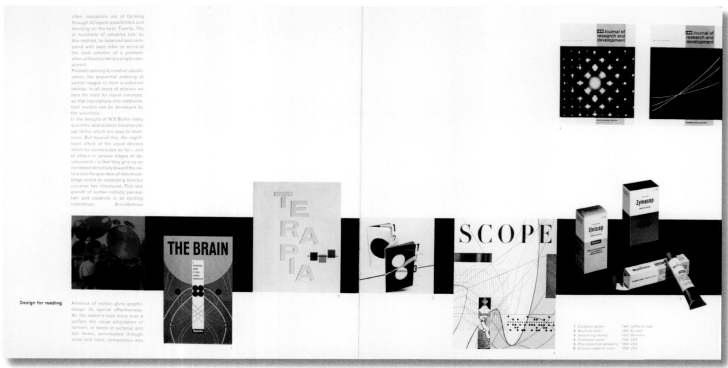

Image 9.8
Inside pages, *Will Burtin: Visual Aspects* brochure.

2nd row
Image 9.9
Inside pages, *Will Burtin: Visual Aspects* brochure, showing Burtin's proposed Eastman Kodak Company building for the 1964-65 World's Fair in New York.

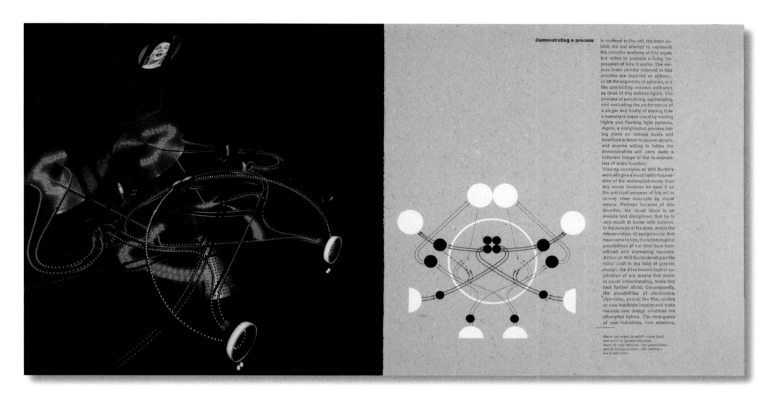

9.3.2
The Communication of Knowledge Exhibition (1971)

In 1971, Burtin received the Medalist Award from the American Institute of Graphic Arts (AIGA), the Professional Organization for Design. Concurrent with the receipt of this prestigious award, Burtin designed a major retrospective exhibition of his career titled, *The Communication of Knowledge* at New York City's former AIGA Gallery. Through 41 modular panels (24 x 24 in.), the exhibition showcased a selection of images that illustrated Burtin's long and successful design career, combining text and full-size photographs and diagrams. As a summary of his major accomplishments, it articulated his philosophy about what he characterized as "designs for mass communication in the science era."[18]

A visual system of three key colors–black, orange and white–organized the material. (see images 9.12 to 9.26.) Clusters of thematically related panels displayed key aspects of Burtin's professional practice: some showcased key projects (panels 5, 6 and 7), while others provided a window into his problem-solving process (panels 12 and 13). Particularly on panel 12, *The chart is visual knowledge*, Burtin invited the viewer inside his unique design process. This panel gave a holistic view into the visual development of two different projects: the visual page plan for an issue of *Fortune* magazine and an evolutionary sequence of approaches to the science of brain research.

Three panels were devoted to clarifying the aims of visual communication itself (panels 15, 16 and 20); another explained what the communication of new knowledge involved (panel 34); and others described emerging simple and complex problems of the time (panels 21, 30 and 32). Burtin also displayed the impact of creating learning tools to promote visual understanding for education (panels 35 and 36) and the idea of "systems thinking" (panels 37 and 38).[19]

With this exhibition, Burtin intended to show how design could foster participation, build curiosity, make complexity more understandable and contribute to the finding of new insights. Many of his major career accomplishments were presented, giving viewers a clear sense of this unique man, his thoughts and his unique approach to design.

Left
Image 9.10
Overview, *The Communication of Knowledge* exhibition, 1971.

Above
Image 9.11
Will Burtin at his studio, c. 1971.

Image 9.12
Panel 1: Opening panel, *The Communication of Knowledge* exhibition.

Image 9.13
Panel 2: Opening panel, *The Communication of Knowledge* exhibition.

Image 9.14
Panel 5: *Life begins: the basic cell.*

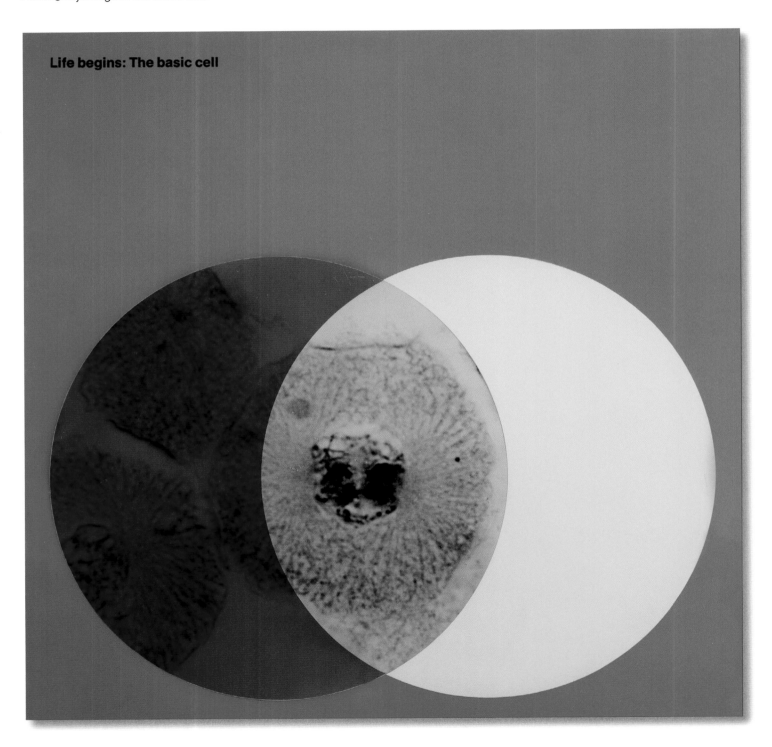

Life begins: The basic cell

Image 9.15
Panel 12: *The chart is visual knowledge.*

The chart is visual knowledge

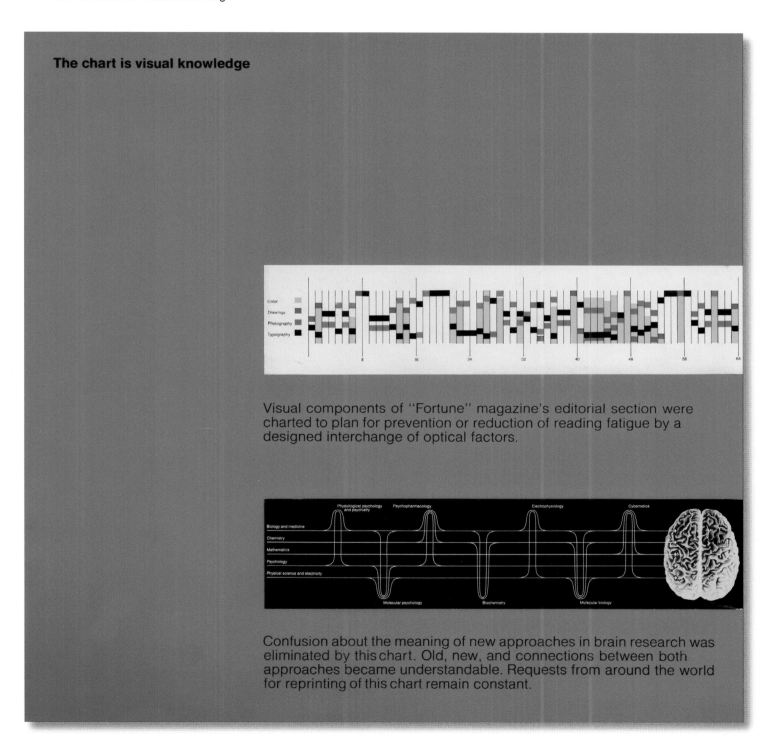

Visual components of "Fortune" magazine's editorial section were charted to plan for prevention or reduction of reading fatigue by a designed interchange of optical factors.

Confusion about the meaning of new approaches in brain research was eliminated by this chart. Old, new, and connections between both approaches became understandable. Requests from around the world for reprinting of this chart remain constant.

Image 9.16
Panel 13: *Design saves time.*

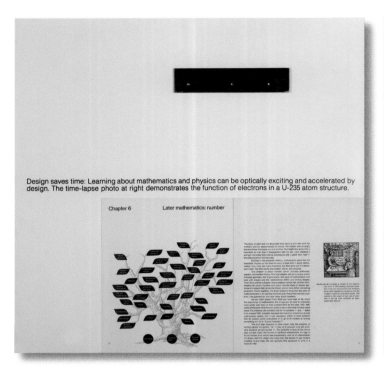

Image 9.17
Panel 14: Photo showing the function of electrons in a U-235 atom structure.

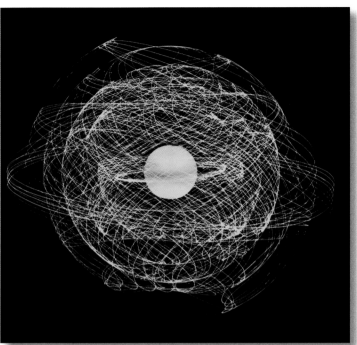

Image 9.18
Panel 15: *Communication: bridges between brains.*

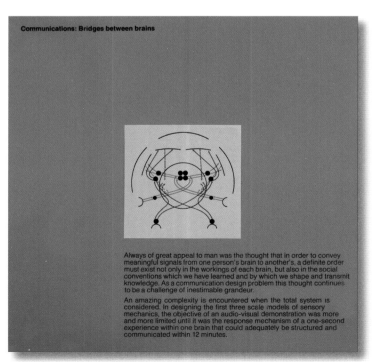

Image 9.19
Panel 20: *New knowledge.*

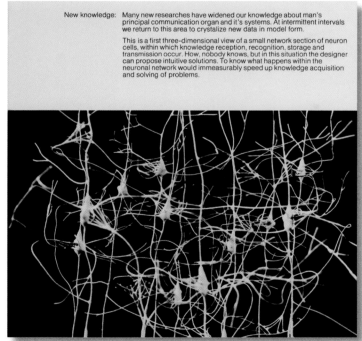

Image 9.20
Panel 24: Photographic evidence of chromosomal structures.

Photographic evidences of chromosomal structures and events are difficult to understand without a visual concept such as the completed model at right.

The electron-micrographs show two types of long chromosome chains and one greatly magnified section of one chain in the act of puffing. The "pipe cleaner" model, lower left, visualizes a chromosome chain.

The X-ray diffraction photo, lower right, proves that a double-helical strand of DNA is wound around a protein molecule (white ring), represented in the model by long aluminum tubes.

Image 9.21
Panel 29: *Saving human time: a design objective*

Image 9.22
Panel 33: *The transparent book.*

The transparent book

informs instantly: The 1931 "Spiegelglas" catalog and the 1971 "a new world" brochure on environment control (IBM) have this in common: each reveals instantly and reminds constantly of its total contents, without hindering absorption and reading concentration.

Aside from an interplay between solid and transparent components there is also a thematic widening of interest that changes from vista to vista — or page to page. The larger pictorial triangles will be printed also on separate self-adhesive paper so that the reader can assemble his own new world on a pre-folded icosahedron as a game or learning tool or memory test.

Image 9.23
Panel 36: *The design of education.*

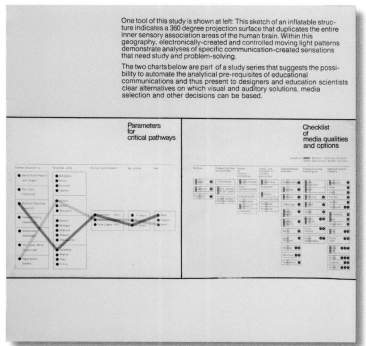

One tool of this study is shown at left: This sketch of an inflatable structure indicates a 360 degree projection surface that duplicates the entire inner sensory association areas of the human brain. Within this geography, electronically-created and controlled moving light patterns demonstrate analyses of specific communication-created sensations that need study and problem-solving.

The two charts below are part of a study series that suggests the possibility to automate the analytical pre-requisites of educational communications and thus present to designers and education scientists clear alternatives on which visual and auditory solutions, media selection and other decisions can be based.

Image 9.24
Panel 25: Image of *Genes in Action* exhibition.

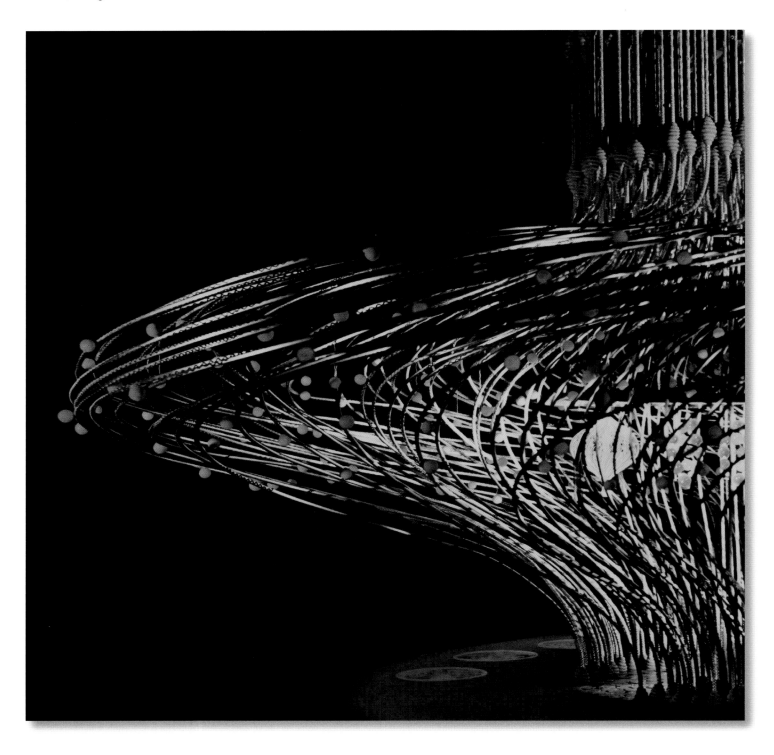

Image 9.25
Panel 25: Image of *Genes in Action* exhibition.

Image 9.26
Panel 30: *Automated audio-visual information dispenser.*

Automated audio-visual information dispenser, to be used at sales conventions, technical conferences and educational meetings.

Purpose:
1. To reduce annual publishing expenses from 32 brochures to eight — cutting reading time from 60 to 15 hours

2. To inform, through eight audio-visual performances of three minutes each, about a new synthetic basic material and its new properties

3. To increase the attentive range of the viewer by cross-relating, for example, automotive with qualifications of ship builders, aviation or environmental health

4. To make learning about the flexibility of a manufacturing process and the ensuing versatility of end products an instant and enjoyable experience.

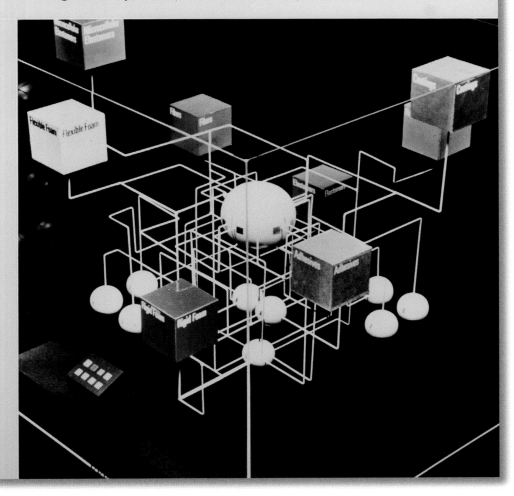

NOTES

1   Will Burtin, "On Science and Education"
    (unpublished manuscript, circa 1964), 5,
    Will Burtin Papers, 13.5–13.7,
    Cary Graphic Design Archive, RIT.

2   Ibid.

3   Richard Buchanan, "Wicked Problems in Design Thinking,"
    Design Issues 8, no. 2 (Spring 1992): 9, https://web.mit.edu/
    jrankin/www/engin_as_lib_art/Design_thinking.pdf.

4   Burtin, "On Science," 2.

5   Burtin, "Enough" (unpublished manuscript, 1970), 5,
    Will Burtin Papers, 94.8–94.9,

    Cary Graphic Design Archive, RIT.

6   Burtin, "A Program in Print: Upjohn and Design" *Print* 9, no. 5
    (insert, May/June 1955); also in Will Burtin Papers, 77.5,
    Cary Graphic Design Archive, RIT.

7   Ibid., 5.

8   Ibid.

9   Buchanan, "Wicked."

10 Sheila Pontis, *Making Sense of Field Research:
    A Practical Guide for Information Designers*
    (Oxfordshire, UK: Routledge, 2018).

11 Burtin, "A Program," 5.

12 Philip B. Meggs, *A History of Graphic Design*, 3rd ed.
    (New York: John Wiley, 1998).

13 Eric Siegel, "Too Big, Too Small, Too Slow, Too Abstract:
    Exhibiting Modern Science," *Exhibitionist* 27, no. 2
    (Fall 2008): 22, https://static1.squarespace.com static/
    58fa260a725e25c4f30020f3/t/59499b72f7e0abeec2b950b4/
    1497996195827/6+EXH_fall08_Too+Big+Too+Small+Too+Slow+Too+
    Abstract-Exhibiting+Modern+Science_Siegel_Baker_Martin.pdf.

14 Flora Lysen, "Blinking Brains, Corporate Spectacle and the
    Atom Man: Visual Aspects of Science at the Stedelijk Museum
    Amsterdam (1962)," *Stedelijk Studies* 2 (Spring 2015): 2,
    http://www.stedelijkstudies.com/journal/blinking-brains-
    corporate-spectacle-and-the-atom-man/.

15 Burtin, Roy Tillotson, Dr. A. Garrard Macleod and
    Bruce MacKenzie, *Will Burtin: Visual Aspects of Science*
    (exhibition brochure, 1962), Will Burtin Papers, 17.4–17.6, 17.7–17.8,
    and 83.9–84.2, Cary Graphic Design Archive, RIT: last page.

16 Ibid.

17 Ibid., 1.

18 Burtin, "Communication of Knowledge" (1971), exhibit panel 3,
    Will Burtin Papers, Boxes 248–261+,
    Cary Graphic Design Archive, RIT.

19 Burtin, "Communication."

Below
Diagram 10.1
Will Burtin's diagram adapted from *Integration* brochure, representing his understanding of the designer's role and the component parts of the design process, 1949.

Right
Diagram 10.2
Will Burtin's diagram adapted from *Integration* brochure, showing a conceptual representation of four realities involved in the visualization of scientific knowledge: science, man, space, light, 1949.

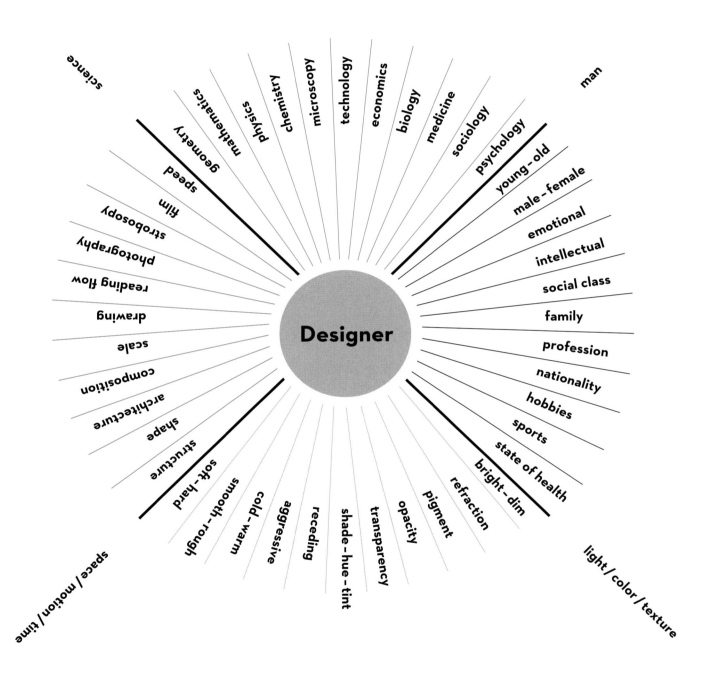

CHAPTER 10

Education

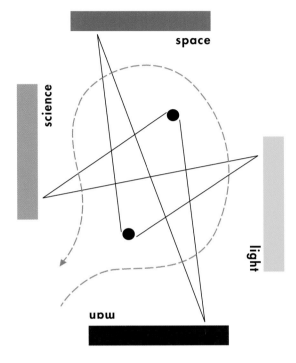

space

science

light

man

10.1
Enhancing Comprehension and Communication

Concurrent with his professional practice, Burtin was deeply interested in education, a commitment that may have emerged from the fact that he was deprived of a full formal education because of the limitations he endured growing up during World War I. He was determined to help shape and train future generations of design professionals, and he strongly believed that the use of visualizations could improve education–that is, the teaching and learning process.

While teaching and designing commercially, Burtin also organized international design conferences, thus contributing to design education and enabling him to interact with other influential designers and scientists to discuss new directions for design. Design historians like Philip Meggs[1] now view Burtin's conferences, *Vision 65*[2] and *Vision 67*[3], as seminal events for design professional practice, because they demonstrated the need for interdisciplinary collaboration and initiated dialogue between professionals from several backgrounds. Burtin also wrote extensively about the role of design, education and communication in the changing world:

> Without a thorough recognition of–and more adequate preparations for dealing with–immediate and long-range consequences of our rapid and often violent social and cultural transformation through the design of a better education, the chances of the young to develop through the confusion and contradiction of change to a more stable synthesis of man, technological evolution and nature are slim.[4]

His solution was to advocate for better training for future generations, to enable them to combine the systematic thinking and rigor of science with the creativity and visual repertoire of design. Today this approach is increasingly becoming the foundation of information design education.

10.2
Rethinking Information Design Education Through a Scientific Lens

Future design educators, according to Burtin, will need to adapt to the new complexities of society by incorporating a scientific approach to solving problems into the design curricula. This approach will "provide education with a bold and new incentive so that young people and teachers [could] respond vigorously to creative opportunities on the many new levels of a new reality."[5] Future design professionals will need to be equipped with the necessary skills and tools to tackle emerging new problems. As Burtin pointed out in the late 1960s, "The social, psychological, technical, political and aesthetic nature and urgency of these problems demand a new and critical attitude toward personal and professional responsibility as well as toward education."[6] In line with Burtin's ideas, Peter Crnokrak, professor at Berlin's University of Applied Sciences Europe, stated that a scientific approach would benefit more creative fields.[7] Burtin wrote that design education should "make [students] aware and prepare them for the fundamental change from the non-scientific to the science era–the new human environment."[8]

Through a design education with a science focus, students can learn how to conceive solutions to problems on many levels and acquire the necessary skills to build those solutions. The first step toward developing this approach is to rethink the current state of design education, both in general and regarding information design in particular. Following Burtin's suggestions, universities and Art and Design schools could focus information design education on providing the framework and tools "to train a creative mind to *solve* communication problems instead of merely enhancing them."[9]

In assessing the big picture, design educators Jorge Frascara and Dietmar Winkler argue that "little has changed" in design education. "Is it not strange," they wrote in 2008, "that after fifty years of supposedly outstanding design education taught by graduates from prestigious schools, the contents/quality of design education has not increased or become more sophisticated? Instead, design education has been compacted and condensed."[10] While the quality of design education may not have increased dramatically in the last decade, new design programs, courses and cross-disciplinary classes have emerged, including the Information Experience Design graduate programs at Royal College of Art in London and at Pratt Institute in New York; the Information Design and Data Visualization graduate program at Northeastern University in Boston; and the Design for Understanding class at Princeton University in New Jersey.

10.2.1
Skills and Knowledge for Information Designers

In the 1960s and until his death in 1972, Burtin wrote extensive memoranda to the Art School at Pratt Institute in New York and the School of Design at the California Institute of the Arts, sharing his vision on education, and especially his ideal of a design department that would teach a program on what he called, "Visual Communications."[11] His perspective for this program was rooted in "new teaching principles and practices," building the underpinnings of a more scientific approach to design, in contrast to the traditional artistic approach of teaching and learning. The program structure, objectives, methods and class distribution described in Burtin's writings meet the needs of today's information design education as outlined, for example, by Inge Gobert and Johan van Looveren[12] in their 2014 book, *Thoughts on Designing Information*, and by Frascara[13] in his 2015 book, *Information Design as Principled Action*. Gobert and van Looveren's book includes the thoughts of Tim Fendley, Andrew Vande Moere, Gerlinde Schuller and 16 other renowned international designers working on a range of project types (information design, data visualization, editorial design, interaction design and environmental design) who describe as essential many of the key skills required by Burtin of his design students.[14]

We summarize Burtin's thoughts on a new visual communication program, reported in his memoranda, as follows:

Mindset

The core facet is the thinking process. Students must have "a flexible and well-organized mind to enable them to:

- Distinguish the real truth in a blurred and colored presentation
- Abstract its essential points
- Translate these points, in order of importance, into a coherent solution. It is quite possible, in fact, that if [they are] able to make a very clear summarized statement about [their] commission, [they] will have solved half [the] problem."[15]

This is in line with what Einstein famously stated concerning the relevance of allocating enough time to first think about a problem before moving forward to actually solving it: "If I had an hour to solve a problem and my life depended on the solution, I would spend the first fifty-five minutes determining the proper question to ask, for once I know the proper question, I could solve the problem in less than five minutes."[16] Practicing this mindset early in their careers will help design students develop "skills that enable them to face their professional future with confidence" and gain "an understanding of the interdependence of art and science and enthusiasm for the new horizons which such an understanding is opening to design."[17] In other words, students will regard defining and framing problems as the first step in successfully finding solutions. Making time to thoroughly understand the problem is essential when dealing with complex, unframed challenges.

Broad Knowledge

Like Gobert and van Looveren, Burtin argued that design students must have a deep knowledge of the major developments in science, art and philosophy, and learn skills in related fields such as journalism, writing, statistical data analysis and the theories and technology of various media. Theories from other disciplines can inform design practice and stimulate a rich reservoir of creativity. Particularly, understanding theories from linguistics (e.g., sign theory, rhetoric), education (constructivist pedagogy) or psychology (Gestalt perceptual principles) can contribute greatly to a designer's toolset. These theories can provide a conceptual framework from which to work.

Communication Skills

Due to their unique role as communicators, information designers stand at the center among all the facets of a problem: the information that needs to be relayed, the client, the intended audience, the problem itself, and the tools to be used. Burtin distinguished the role of the designer from that of the artist arguing that, unlike artists–most of whom are concerned with expressing their own inner feelings– visual communication designers were primarily intermediaries in the communication of ideas. Thus, their education must enable them "to understand the language of scientists, artists and officials, so that [they] can translate their thoughts and ideas into visual terms."[18] In order to successfully orchestrate meetings with professionals of various backgrounds, students should learn techniques such as questioning, listening skills, the ability to extract the main ideas from what is said, an instinct for finding connections between what different people are saying, and the facility to help others externalize their thinking.

Visualization Skills

On a problem-solving team, the designer should have the skills to contribute a visualization capability to the effort. A good information designer can make the invisible visible at various stages of the process. At the beginning, he or she can use visual thinking techniques to help the team communicate ideas in the form of rough drawings or sketches; later, these techniques can translate content into an understandable, more refined visual form. To be equipped with a rich repertoire of visual techniques, Burtin wrote, "The student should be trained to reach a thorough understanding ... of the philosophy, forms and techniques of visual communication."[19] Students should learn cognitive and perceptual principles to understand and properly use pre-cognitive visual attributes such as color, shape, value, orientation, proximity and size: the basic components of visual languages.[20] These principles are key to determining when each visual attribute can be used to help distinguish, emphasize or connect information.

Research Skills

Increasing complexity demands that information designers be well-informed about all components of the problem at hand by seeking a deeper understanding of the problem, or hard evidence to support design decisions. Burtin argued that "hit and miss propositions" based on arbitrary decisions were not good, and that instead, a continuous progress based on insight and understanding was desirable. Students "should not expect to attend school for two or three months, gain some knowledge, and then automatically be an accomplished designer."[21] Design is hard work. The designer who conducts the most solid and compelling research will also create well-conceived solutions. Gobert and van Looveren also point out the need for students to develop skills to collect information and analyze data, in order to "recognize the trends, patterns and motivations that fuel the stories that need to be told."[22] Students should learn a range of research methods, not just how to gather theoretical or academic insights. Skills they need include ethnographic techniques, the ability to ask questions effectively, and a solid grounding in talking with experts and other professionals. Once they have learned research values and techniques, designers should use their creative skills to tailor each method to the particular specifications of a problem.

Organizing Skills

In order to make sense of challenging or disorganized data, information designers work with organizing principles to apply structure to the data by categorizing, grouping, mapping and extracting the relevant from irrelevant information. "Only if they have the ability to select those items of information from which [they] can draw [their] own conclusions," will they be able to "give form to communication between people."[23] Students should master these organizing methods and frameworks to break a complex topic or substance into smaller parts, and to identify key components in the data. Organizing skills are also essential to determining the hierarchical structure of information, and pinpointing the patterns and connections between the different components, categories and levels of information.

Technical Skills

Following the conceptual part of the process, designers need to translate the resulting organized information into a visual form using the most appropriate techniques, perhaps digital tools to create 2D artifacts, or materials to create 3D models. For this step, designers need to embrace the latest technology, programming, tools and materials available to do their job. As Burtin wrote, "Designers should have a range of professional competence by which they can turn from the motions of lights to the collage, from the graph to a motion picture, from a three-dimensional model to a television sequence, from color and sound to letter forms."[24] After students first gain an awareness of the rich repertoire of techniques and materials that they can work with, they can then go deeper into some or all of the specific techniques.

Burtin also wanted his design students to have "an appreciation of the social function and special responsibility of design," being aware of the impact that they would have on users and the environment, and taking into account the ethical considerations involved in their work.[25] He felt that information design education should encourage "good self-discipline" and self-reflection as essential requirements. But, at the same time, it must be "flexible enough to continually reflect the changes in modern communication."[26]

Image 10.1
Will Burtin with young student examining
The Cell exhibition elements, New York, 1959.

10.3
Educating through Information Design

The analysis of Burtin's projects presented in the previous chapters highlights the close relationship between information design and the learning process. His projects contributed to education in several ways. For example, his exhibitions and editorial projects brought science closer to universities, high schools and medical colleges (they asked the Upjohn Company for permission to build cell models from his construction drawings and photographs). Furthermore, biology textbooks used photographs from *The Cell* exhibition as cover and text illustrations to support student learning; and the US Army Air Force and similar organizations realized shorter training times and more effective performance because of his work.[27]

The strong impact of information design in education is explicitly articulated in Burtin's 1966 design for the Pantheon/Random House book *The Pantheon Story of Mathematics for Young People*[28] by James T. Rogers, which helped youngsters understand basic arithmetic concepts. The book's cover sets the tone for the content: "The development of mathematical thought from the finger-counting of primitive man to the electronic computer." (see image 10.2.) The opening front flap stated, "With remarkable clarity and a bold, stimulating approach, James T. Rogers and Will Burtin have accomplished a most difficult task: They have telescoped the vast, ever expanding world of mathematics into a lucid and fascinating account of its gradual development." The back cover credits Burtin and adds, "The mathematical basis for the beauty of the physical world has inspired the union of text and illustrations in this book." (see image 10.3.)

The book was large in size (11.25 × 9 in.) and organized into nine chapters, discussing a range of topics, from the contributions of the Greeks to mathematics today. The use of Helvetica type and the orange color, along with clearly understandable photographic images, diagrams, charts, graphs, and visual metaphors, creates a visual learning experience that brings the content alive for its youthful audience. For example, the concept of multiplication is explained with a visual metaphor–orange loaves of bread as units–to make it more tangible to young readers and motivate them to learn. (see image 10.4.) Similarly, chapter 3 of the book explains the evolution of geometry with a diagram showing a geometric construction similar to what the Greeks used to calculate unknown dimensions of a triangle from known dimensions, such as the lengths of sides and size of angles. (see image 10.5 detail.)

For Burtin, the visualization of information was paramount to explain complex concepts, as his projects exemplify, but also to support learning and improve education. *The Pantheon Story of Mathematics for Young People* illustrates Burtin's view, and how the use of visualization could enhance teaching and learning. Today visualizations are a core ingredient in information design education and instructional contexts.

Image 10.2
Cover, *The Pantheon Story of Mathematics for Young People* book, 1966.

James T. Rogers · The Pantheon Story of Mathematics for young people

The
development
of mathematical thought
from
the finger-counting
of primitive man
to
the electronic
computer.

Image 10.3
Back cover, *The Pantheon Story of Mathematics for Young People* book, 1966.

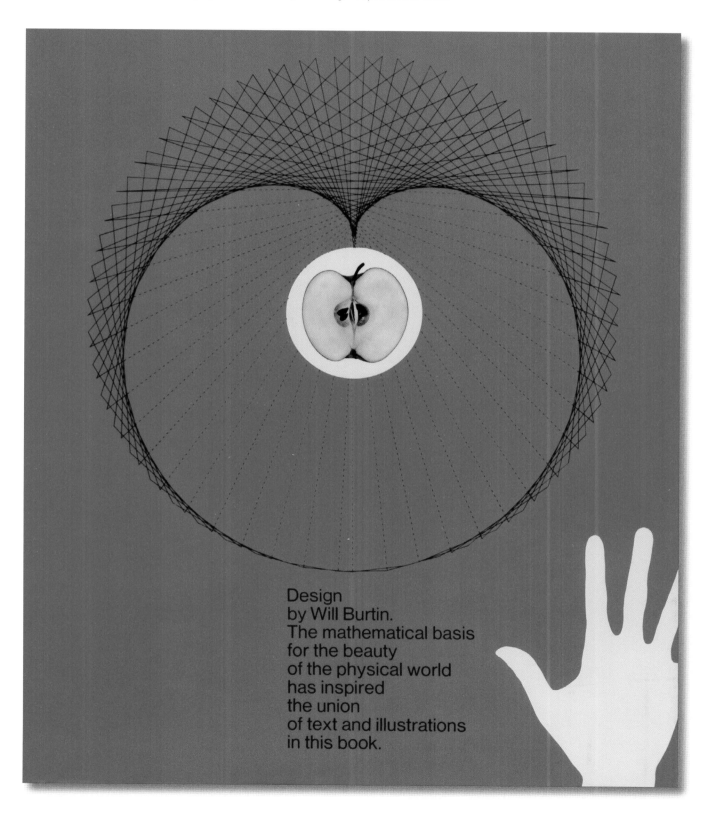

Design
by Will Burtin.
The mathematical basis
for the beauty
of the physical world
has inspired
the union
of text and illustrations
in this book.

Images 10.4 and 10.5
Inside pages, *The Pantheon Story* book.

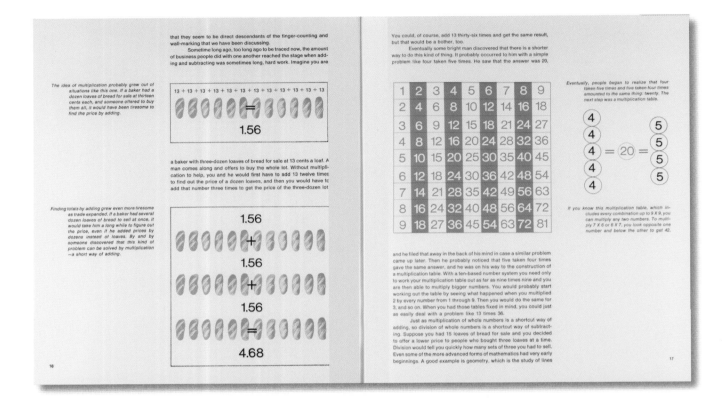

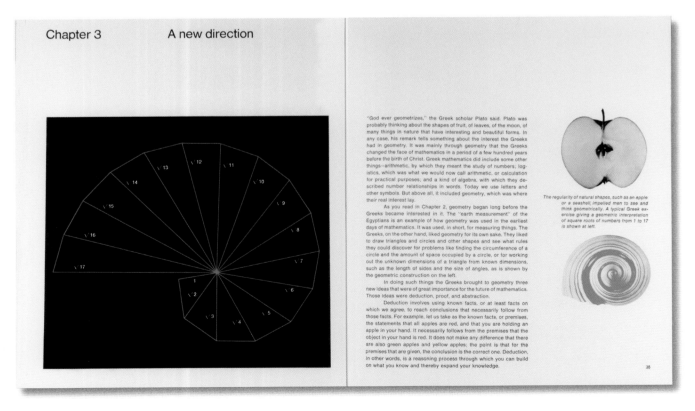

Image 10.5 Detail
Diagram from *The Pantheon Story* book.

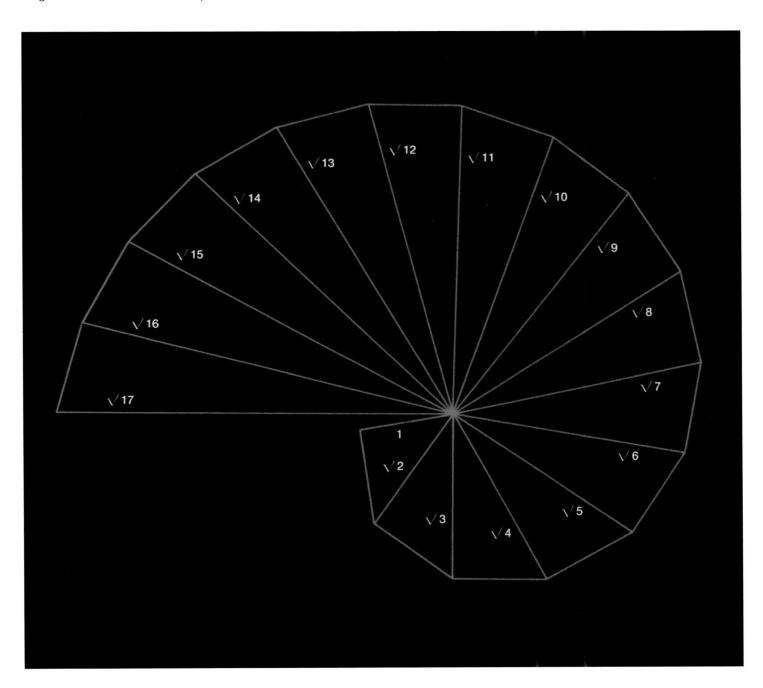

NOTES

1 Philip B. Meggs, *A History of Graphic Design*, 3rd ed.
(New York: John Wiley, 1998).

2 *Vision 65: World Congress on New Challenges to
Human Communication* was held at
Southern Illinois University (US) from October 21–23, 1965.
A diverse group of international designers, architects,
theorists, historians, futurists and others attended the
conference to discuss the challenges of communications
as a result of technological and social developments.
Many of those who attended felt that the conference
was historic in itself because of the power of the range
of diverse speakers including Marshall McLuhan,
Buckminster Fuller, Armin Hofmann and many others,
which brought a great richness and diversity of
perspectives about design.

3 *Vision 67: Survival and Growth* took place in New York at
New York University from October 19–22, 1967. Similarly to
Vision 65, speakers and presenters came from different
countries and backgrounds generating thoughtful discussions,
Speakers included Umberto Eco, Ken Garland,
Arthur Funkhauser, and Kurt Blum. Patterned on the the first
conference, it was less effective due to overall quality of
speakers and general attitudes of political unrest at the time.

4 Will Burtin to Dr. Herbert Blau, Provost,
California Institute of the Arts, "Thoughts about Function and
Program of a School of Design" (circa 1970), 1,
Will Burtin Papers, 97.6, Cary Graphic Design Archive, RIT.

5 Ibid.

6 Ibid., 2.

7 Inge Gobert and Johan van Looveren,
Thoughts on Designing Information
(Zurich: Lars Müller, 2014), 38–47.

8 Burtin, "Communication of Knowledge" (1971),
exhibit panel 3, Will Burtin Papers, Boxes 248–261+,
Cary Graphic Design Archive, RIT.

9 Burtin, "On Science and Education"
(unpublished manuscript, circa 1964), 1,
Will Burtin Papers, 13.5–13.7,
Cary Graphic Design Archive, RIT.

10 Jorge Frascara and Dietmar Winkler,
"On Design Research,"
Design Research Quarterly 3, no. 3 (July 2008): 4,
https://www.dropbox.com/s/tr9b7727go98nw6/
200807%20DRQ.pdf?dl=0.

11 Burtin to Dr. Blau; Burtin to Dean Albert Christ-Janer,
The Art School, Pratt Institute, "Memorandum on the
Organization of a Design Department which Teaches
'Visual Communications'" (circa 1959),
Will Burtin Papers, 96.9–97.3 (box 17: folder 3 of 8),
Cary Graphic Design Archive, RIT.

12 Gobert and van Looveren, *Thoughts*.

13 Frascara, *Information Design as Principled Action: Making Information Accessible, Relevant, Understandable, and Usable* (Champaign, IL: Common Ground Publishing, 2015).

14 Gobert and van Looveren, *Thoughts*.

15 Burtin, "Notes on The Visual Communication Designer" (unpublished notes, The Art School, Pratt Institute, 1963), 1, Will Burtin Papers, 96.9–97.3, Cary Graphic Design Archive, RIT.

16 Tina Seelig, *inGenius. A Crash Course on Creativity*, reprint (San Francisco: HarperOne, 2015), 10.

17 Burtin to Christ-Janer, 1.

18 Burtin, "Notes on The Visual," 1.

19 Burtin to Christ-Janer, 1.

20 Jacques Bertin, *Semiology of Graphics: Diagrams, Networks, Maps* (Redlands, CA: Esri Press, 2010).

21 Burtin, "Theory of Design Course Lectures" (Lecture 1, February 20, 1947), 2, Will Burtin Papers, 96.7, Cary Graphic Design Archive, RIT.

22 Gobert and van Looveren, *Thoughts*, 152.

23 Burtin, "Notes on The Visual," 1.

24 Burtin, "Reflections on Graphic Design" (unpublished manuscript, 1966), 18, Will Burtin Will Burtin Papers, 93.5, Cary Graphic Design Archive, RIT.

25 Burtin to Christ-Janer, 1.

26 Burtin, "Notes on the Visual," 2.

27 Burtin, "Observations on the Development of the Brain Model" (unpublished manuscript, April 10, 1960), Will Burtin Papers, 12.3, Cary Graphic Design Archive, RIT.

28 James T. Rogers, *The Pantheon Story of Mathematics for Young People* (New York: Pantheon Books, 1966).

Diagram 11.1
Diagram summarizing Will Burtin's scientific approach
to visual communication discussed in the book.

Will Burtin's Scientific Approach to Visual Communication

Conceptual Design

1 Understand Problem and Audience
Talk with experts, and get familiar with audience

2 Define and Frame Problem
Determine what makes the problem hard to understand

UNDERSTANDING BARRIERS FOR SCIENTIFIC CONTENT
- Too **small**, hard to see
- Too **abstract**, hard to imagine
- Too **many components**, hard to identify each component

3 Understand Content
Gain experience and familiarity with content

4 Develop Idea and Design Concept
Select appropriate sensemaking strategies
to make content more accessible
and generate ideas to communicate content

INFORMATION DESIGN STRATEGIES
- Increase scale and show **hidden information**
- Explain **how something works**, not how it looks
- Make the **abstract tangible** and the **unfamiliar familiar**

Prototype Design

5 Visual Translation
Identify appropriate materials to create models
and build prototype

CHAPTER 11

Recommendations and Information Design Imperatives

11.1

Being an Information Designer

For information design to evolve as a field and move forward, today's designers, modeling Will Burtin, should be "strongly against the type of thinking that has been prevailing in schools generally–that just because someone learns to connect arrows and eyes together, it is assumed that person is a modern designer and an expert on every conceivable problem," able to find a "creative shortcut" to solve a problem.[1] For Burtin, being an information designer meant thinking of each problem as "a comprehensive" design work, involving purposeful direction, confidence and patience. It meant giving "much time to recognize a problem, then to become familiar with its inner structure."[2] Both *dedication* and *cooperative work* are essential qualities for the designer to "look critically beyond a momentary, good solution and [instead] strive for the one that appears most eloquent in terms of the audience to whom those structures are directed," and to "coordinate the work of many specialists to solve these problems."[3] An information designer must have a strong sense of ethics, as well as the commitment and determination to seek and convey understanding.

11.2

Bringing the Past into the Present of Information Design

A review of Burtin's career and work, asks this question: What specific guidance can we glean from this man and his history? We have already analyzed Burtin's work through seven dimensions of information design. Here, we present seven core tasks related to the current state of the field and reflect upon how Burtin's experience could provide relevant guidance to information designers today.

Seven Core Tasks

1 **Information designers often lack a thorough understanding of problem situations, so they struggle to properly frame challenges.**

How can information designers frame and understand complex challenges?

2 **Complex projects involve both disorganized information and information coming from an assortment of sources and different media.**

How can information designers make sense of large amounts of dispersed information?

Ask questions and play an active role

Traditionally, design education positioned the designer in a passive role. Designers received a commission from a client and went to the studio to work on a solution, coming up with three options from which the client could choose. But, as Burtin told his students, "technical skills play less and less of a role than the versatility of the mind. It is important to have a combination of both. We should have emotion as well as intellectual ability."[4] Currently, more and more, information designers identify and frame problems themselves, and then formulate design briefs. Burtin's hunger for learning motivated him to ask questions and become deeply immersed in each project. Today, asking basic and critical questions throughout the process is a must-have skill.

Gain familiarity with cognitive processes and perceptual principles

Effective information design supports cognitive processes involved in making sense of both everyday activities and complex situations or subjects, because information is translated into visual forms that are in line with perceptual principles. Understanding these processes and principles will help designers to be more aware of the job and to better understand why some design decisions work and others don't.

Burtin found that an effective means of conveying the complexity of scientific phenomena was by having the audience become involved in the design process. Working together with the audience will help designers to determine what information is relevant to keep and what is not to make the topic more accessible. Once these priorities are accomplished, designers can then determine the most appropriate media and language to connect with the audience and communicate the message effectively. Walk-in exhibitions accomplished this goal. Burtin's exhibitions "followed the principle that such three-dimensional structures, scaled to human size and human motion," would assure "an orderly progression of information."[5] Three-dimensional exhibitions create an interactive experience for visitors, who can look ahead, back, down and around the space, assimilating information at their own pace, and deciding when to skip over certain details. Burtin felt that walk-in exhibitions gave people an intense and flexible learning journey, hard to mirror with any other medium. Today, new technologies, such as augmented reality or artificial intelligence, have opened up the range of possibilities in which people can interact with and be involved in the learning experience.

3 While a solution to a design problem may look good, it may not respond to the audience's needs, or be used or experienced by them as intended.

How can information designers gain a deeper understanding of their audiences?

4 Information designers deal with problems that demand specialized knowledge in non-design subjects.

How can information designers make informed decisions?

Put people first

Design decisions are frequently made based on personal tastes, past experiences, assumptions, or knowledge obtained during client meetings, all of which can result in ineffective solutions. Instead, decisions should respond to the needs of the intended audience and to the specifications of the project at hand. This is why a human-centered approach is increasingly being adopted in information design professional practice, and often the budget includes an allocation for user studies.

But in most cases, these studies are carried out only to test prototypes or to evaluate the effectiveness of solutions once they have been implemented (later part of the process). However, projects need to begin with a thorough understanding of the audience, and, in their earliest stages, allocate time to conduct user studies to identify people's needs and behaviors. For Burtin, learning firsthand how his audience behaved, and identifying those aspects of a problem-situation that weren't working or were harder to understand, were essential tasks, to the point that he would routinely put himself in the audience's shoes. After understanding the problem itself, understanding the audience was his next step. Sometimes it is necessary to accomplish the latter to understand the former.

Work in collaboration with content experts and gain familiarity with the problem topic

While solving a problem, information designers need to make a wide range of decisions. As Burtin stressed on many occasions, information designers need to work closely with content experts to become deeply familiar with the subject matter of a project. Today, to gain this familiarity, in some cases, designers define, plan and conduct research studies. The use of ethnographic methods, such as contextual interviews and observations with content experts, are commonplace in design professional practice. This doesn't mean that designers become scientists, but rather they examine a design project from many angles and from various perspectives, and gather firsthand insights from many people. Insights and learnings help designers make design decisions based on evidence, rather than on only their experience and assumptions.

5 **Information designers are rapidly moving away from working by themselves to working in cross-disciplinary teams.**

How can information designers ensure that all team members are on the same page?

6 **Even though outcomes may reflect mastery in visual integration, some design decisions can be misleading or not communicate accurate information.**

How can information designers ensure that design decisions are ethical and do not confuse the audience's understanding of the message?

Become facilitators of dialogue by using visual means
Professionals in many disciplines speak their own languages. As information designers work with team members from different backgrounds, they need to develop the skills they will need to share thoughts, articulate ideas, and facilitate dialogue among the team members, making sure that all members depart from meetings with the same understandings. Burtin first faced this challenge when he was working as an art director, communicating with peer designers, content experts and board members. Later, when working on his exhibitions, he faced it again. His interactions with others resulted in the creation of sketches or models that enhance communication and facilitate understanding.

Ensure transparency and accuracy and think about the broader implications of the work
As professionals working to communicate messages, facts and processes, information designers have an important ethical responsibility. Even when the data does not allow the creation of a "visually appealing" design, designers should maintain transparency and content accuracy. Changing one number for the sake of a design solution can lead to communicating misleading information, and eventually to audience misunderstanding or making the wrong decisions. Burtin vigorously called upon designers to use their skills to create "high ethical value," and asserted that, throughout their careers, designers "should strive to enrich lives, so a better understanding and view of life can occur."[6] Similarly, information designers need to be aware of the broader implications of their work.

Conduct evaluative studies and externalize the thinking process

Most designers, early in their careers, learn the technical side of the field, especially the mastery of digital skills. For many of them, turning on their computers and beginning to design are the very first steps in the process. Consequently, these designers often make arbitrary decisions and rely on their own inspiration and expertise without fully understanding why one decision was better than another. This could result in either an effective solution or a poor solution Burtin, on the other hand, strongly emphasized the role of process and of understanding the problem before executing any ideas. By sharing their thinking with team members, testing ideas with an audience and reflecting on their understanding of what is needed, information designers would become more involved in the process and develop a better understanding of the impact of their decisions.[7] Building on Burtin's own notions of process and workflow would help such information designers. Both being equally involved in the commercial production and marketing aspects of a design project and in "the prior stages of invention, of scientific research and of resources development, on a broad level"[8] are critical.

We live in a time of constant change where everything is interconnected. Designers who are unaware of this current context will be unequipped to develop a successful solution. Understanding the reasons behind social, cultural, economic, technological and political changes has become paramount to addressing complex problems.[9] As Burtin told his students in 1949, good designers need to understand design history to fully comprehend the current design landscape.[10] The same advice would help current designers and students to make sense of what is happening now.

Throughout this book, we used Burtin's scientific approach to communicate knowledge visually, introduced in chapter 3 and exemplified throughout his projects (chapters 4 to 10), as a framework for designers to pay greater attention to conceptual design, which is needed to deal with complex challenges. Additionally, the analysis of his work through the lens of seven core dimensions of information design sheds light on how Burtin's approach could support information designers' process today.

As we stressed in the first chapter, the increased need for understanding the world makes the work of information designers more necessary than ever today *(Dimension 1: Purpose)*. Rather than approaching new challenges as framed problems and focusing on how they ought to be solved, designers should follow Burtin's philosophy and start each new project as a "blank slate,"[11] by focusing on its potential for learning and understanding, while working on defining its boundaries *(Dimension 2: Problem)*.

Working with a scientific approach to design in professional practice would add rigor, and help designers make more informed design decisions, as it emphasizes the role of understanding the audience and subject matter of the problem before starting work on a solution *(Dimension 3: Audience)*. It would encourage designers to work in teams with professionals from other domains, fostering cross-disciplinary dialogue *(Dimension 4: Approach)* where designers translate team members' thoughts and ideas into visual form. The quality and success of Burtin's projects illustrate the core principles of effective information design *(Dimension 5: Outcome)*: clearly defining the problem, well-defined information hierarchies, logic visual structure, and appropriate use of visual language and materials. The closer look at Burtin's design process, through each of the five Process Boxes, provides a detailed view into the tasks and activities involved in information design *(Dimension 6: Practice)* and the complexity of the work needed to create relevant and effective solutions.

Burtin's philosophy comes through strongly via his writings and rich contributions to design education, as well as his commitment to better prepare the next generation of designers for the changing world *(Dimension 7: Education)*. For Burtin, teaching design was "an opportunity to fire the creative imagination of a restless generation of people" and equip them with the mindset and skills to "discover solutions to problems on many levels of existence."[12] Today, his vision and ideas about how to teach visual communication, discussed in the previous chapter, can help shape the future of information design education.

The career, accomplishments and ideas of Will Burtin invite re-examination. His personal and professional journey to facilitating understanding of complexity through his designs shaped the way he saw the world and how he thought about and solved problems. Understanding Burtin's journey today could help shape the future of many information designers and have a marked effect on the quality of visualized information.

NOTES

1 Will Burtin, "Theory of Design Course Lectures"
(Lecture 1, February 20, 1947), 2,
Will Burtin Papers, 96.7, Cary Graphic Design Archive,
Rochester Institute of Technology.

2 Burtin, "A Program in Print: Upjohn and Design"
Print 10, no. 4 (insert, May/June 1955): 5; also in
Will Burtin Papers, 77.5, Cary Graphic Design Archive, RIT.

3 Ibid.

4 Burtin, Lecture 1, 11.

5 Burtin, "Program," 4.

6 Burtin, Lecture 1, 8.

7 Steven Heller and Rick Landers,
Infographic Designers' Sketchbooks
(New York: Princeton Architectural Press, 2014);
Jorge Frascara, *Information Design as Principled Action:*
Making Information Accessible, Relevant, Understandable,
and Usable (Champaign, IL: Common Ground, 2015);
Sheila Pontis and Michael Babwahsingh,
"Start with the Basics: Understanding Before Doing"
(symposium paper, *IIID Vision Plus* 2015 proceedings,
Birmingham City University, UK, September 4, 2015), 90–102,
https://www.iiid.net/downloads/IIID-VisionPlus-2015-
Proceedings.pdf.

8 Burtin, "Reflections on Graphic Design"
(unpublished manuscript, 1966), 4,
Will Burtin Papers, 93.5, Cary Graphic Design Archive, RIT.

9 Burtin, Lecture 1.

10 Ibid., 3.

11 Burtin, "Theory of Design Course Lectures"
(Lecture 1, February 20, 1947), 2,
Will Burtin Papers, 96.7, Cary Graphic Design Archive, RIT.

12 Will Burtin to Dr. Herbert Blau,
Provost, California Institute of Art, "Thoughts about Function
and Program of a School of Design" (circa 1970), 1,
Will Burtin Papers, 97.6, Cary Graphic Design Archive, RIT.

Acknowledgments

We would like first to thank Will Burtin. His timeless ideas, work and journey bridge the past and the present and will help guide younger generations of designers and scientists in search of effective ways of communicating science. Many thanks to Bruce Austin, Director, Molly Cort, Managing Editor, Marnie Soom, Design and Marketing Specialist, and Laura Heise, Business Manager at RIT Press for their support along the way; to Patty Cost for editing and Kathleen Smith for copyediting the manuscript. Special thanks as well to Bruce Ian Meader for his help with the design of the book. We also are grateful to the following individuals for their support and encouragement in the realization of this book:

Carol Burtin Fripp

Robert S.P. Fripp

M. Suzanne Remington

Michael Babwahsingh

Elizabeth Lamark

Amelia Hugill Fontanel

Rebecca Simmons

Graciela Salerno

Horacio Pontis

Josh Owen

Steven Galbraith

Edward Nadler

Erica Stoller

Bibliography

A

A Moment at a Concert. Kalamazoo, MI: Upjohn, 1961.
Exhibition brochure. Will Burtin Papers, 67.5–67.6,
Cary Graphic Design Archive,
Rochester Institute of Technology.

Arnold, General Henry H. *This is Your Gun.* Introduction.
Washington, DC: Office of Strategic Services, 1944.
Will Burtin Papers (box 64), Cary Graphic Design Archive, RIT.

Aynsley, Jeremy. "'Gebrauchsgraphik' as an
Early Graphic Design Journal, 1924–1938."
Journal of Design History 5, no. 1 (1992): 53–72.

B

Baer, Kim. *Information Design Workbook:
Graphic Approaches, Solutions, and Inspiration +
30 Case Studies.* Beverly, MA: Rockport, 2008.

Bertin, Jacques. *Semiology of Graphics: Diagrams, Networks,
Maps.* Redlands, CA: Esri Press, 2010.

Brower, Steven. "Design History 101: From Pharma to Fortune,
Designer Will Burtin Has Range."*AIGA: Eye on Design*
(November 12, 2015), https://eyeondesign.aiga.org/from-
pharma-to-fortune-designer-will-burtin-has-range/.

Buchanan, Richard. "Wicked Problems in Design Thinking."
Design Issues 8, no. 2 (Spring 1992): 5–21. https://web.mit.edu/
jrankin/www/engin_as_lib_art/Design_thinking.pdf.

Burgoyne, Patrick. "Will Burtin: Forgotten Master
of Design." *Creative Review* (November 27, 2007),
https://www.creativereview.co.uk/cr-blog/2007/november/
will-burtin-forgotten-master-of-design/

Burtin, Will. "2-D or 3-D?" Unpublished manuscript, 1964.
Will Burtin Papers, 92.5, Cary Graphic Design Archive, RIT.

_____. "A Program in Print: Upjohn and Design." *Print* 9, no. 5
(May/June 1955): 36–60. Also in Will Burtin Papers, 77.5,
Cary Graphic Design Archive, RIT.

_____. "Brain, correspondence." Unpublished draft for
Industrial Design vol. 7 no. 8, August 1960.
Will Burtin Papers, 12.3, Cary Graphic Design Archive, RIT.

_____. "Communication of Knowledge." Exhibit panels, 1971.
Will Burtin Papers, Boxes 248–261+,
Cary Graphic Design Archive, RIT.

_____. "Enough." Unpublished manuscript, 1970.
Will Burtin Papers, 94.8–94.9, Will Burtin Papers,
Cary Graphic Design Archive, RIT.

_____. "From Where to Where?" Foreword in
*Typography–USA.Forum: "What Is New in American
Typography?"* April 18, 1959, Hotel Biltmore, New York City,
by Aaron Burns, et al.
New York: Type Directors Club of New York, 1959.
Cary Graphic Arts Collection, 106609, Wallace Center, RIT.

_____. *Integration–The New Discipline in Design.* A-D Gallery
Exhibit Catalog, 1948. Will Burtin Papers, 55.11–55.12,
Cary Graphic Design Archive, RIT.

_____. *Integration–The New Discipline in Design.* Exhibition
brochure. Chicago: Art Directors Club, 1949. Will Burtin Papers,
55.6 and 90.12–90.13, Cary Graphic Design Archive, RIT.

_____. "Integration, The New Discipline in Design: An Exhibition
by Will Burtin from Nov. 9, 1948 to January 14, 1949."
Graphis 27 (1949): 230–237.

_____. "Man is Responsible for his Environment, project
development." 1971. For exhibition at the *United Nations
Conference on the Human Environment*, Stockholm, June 1972.
Will Burtin Papers, 9.9–9.10, Cary Graphic Design Archive, RIT.

_____. "Notes on The Visual Communication Designer."
Unpublished notes, The Art School, Pratt Institute, 1963. Will
Burtin Papers, 97.2, Cary Graphic Design Archive, RIT.

_____. "Notes on Visual Design." Unpublished notes, n.d. Will
Burtin Papers, 97.3, Cary Graphic Design Archive, RIT.

_____. "Observations on the Development of the Brain Model."
April 10, 1960. Will Burtin Papers, 12.3,
Cary Graphic Design Archive, RIT.

_____. "On Science and Education." Unpublished manuscript,
circa 1964. Will Burtin Papers, 13.5–13.7,
Cary Graphic Design Archive, RIT.

_____. "Reflections on Graphic Design." Unpublished
manuscript, 1966. Will Burtin Papers, 93.5,
Cary Graphic Design Archive, RIT.

_____. "Theory of Design Course Lectures,"
Lecture 1, February 20, 1947. Will Burtin Papers, 96.7,
Cary Graphic Design Archive, RIT.

_____. "Thoughts on Three-Dimensional Science Communications." *Dot Zero* 4 (Summer 1967: World's Fairs): 30-37.

_____ to Caroll E. Casey, Eastman Kodak Company. July 24, 1962. Will Burtin Papers, 6.2, Cary Graphic Design Archive, RIT.

_____ to Dean Albert Christ-Janer, The Art School, Pratt Institute. "Memorandum on the Organization of a Design Department which Teaches 'Visual Communications.'" Circa 1959. Will Burtin Papers, 96.9–97.3 (box 17: folder 3 of 8), Cary Graphic Design Archive, RIT.

_____ to Dr. Herbert Blau, Provost, California Insitute of Art. "Thoughts about Function and Program of a School of Design." Circa 1970. Will Burtin Papers, 97.6, Cary Graphic Design Archive, RIT.

_____ to Dr. Macleod, January 9, 1944. Will Burtin Papers, 98.1, Cary Graphic Design Archive, RIT.

_____ and Lawrence P. Lessing. "Interrelations." *Graphis* 22, vol. 4 (1948): 108–117.

_____, Roy Tillotson, Dr. A. Garrard Macleod and Bruce MacKenzie. *Will Burtin: Visual Aspects of Science.* Exhibition brochure, 1962. Will Burtin Papers, 17.4–17.6, 17.7–17.8, and 83.9–84.2, Cary Graphic Design Archive, RIT.

_____ "Untitled Notes." Unpublished notes, n.d. Will Burtin Papers, 64, Cary Graphic Design Archive, RIT.

C

The Cell: An Exhibit Presenting the Basic Unit of Life. Kalamazoo, MI: Upjohn, circa 1958–1960. Exhibition brochure. Will Burtin Papers, 68.1 and Drawer 55.5–55.6, Cary Graphic Design Archive, RIT.

The Cell. A Scope Monograph on Cytology. Kalamazoo, MI: Upjohn, 1958. Will Burtin Papers, 68.2–68.3, Cary Graphic Design Archive, RIT.

Conley, Chris. "Where are the design methodologists?" *Visible Language* 38, no. 2 (2004): 196–215.

Conway, Rowan, Jeff Masters, and Jake Thorold. "From Design Thinking to Systems Change." London: RSA Action and Research Centre, July 2017. https://www.thersa.org/globalassets/pdfs/reports/rsa_from-design-thinking-to-system-change-report.pdf.

Cross, Nigel. "Designerly Ways of Knowing: Design Discipline versus Design Science." *Design Issues* 17, no. 3 (2001): 49–55, http://oro.open.ac.uk/3281/1/Designerly-_DisciplinevScience.pdf.

F

Foley, James and William Ribarsky. "Next-Generation Data Visualization Tools." In *Scientific Visualization*, by Lawrence J. Rosenblum et al. London Academic Press, 1994, 103–127. https://smartech.gatech.edu/bitstream/handle/1853/3594/94-27.pdf?sequence=1&isAllowed=y.

Francis, M. (2014) *Cognitive celebrity. Albert Einstein was a genius, but he wasn't the only one – why has his name come to mean something superhuman?* (Online Essay) [Available at: https://aeon.co/essays/how-did-albert-einstein-become-the-poster-boy-for-genius- Accessed online 2 February 2016]

Frascara, Jorge. *Information Design as Principled Action: Making Information Accessible, Relevant, Understandable, and Usable.* Champaign, IL: Common Ground, 2015.

Frascara and Dietmar Winkler. "On Design Research." *Design Research Quarterly* 3, no. 3 (July 2008):1–14. https://www.dropbox.com/s/tr9b7727go98nw6/200807%20DRQ.pdf?dl=0

G

Gleick, James. *The Information: A History, a Theory, a Flood.* New York: Pantheon, 2012.

Gobert, Inge and Johan van Looveren. *Thoughts on Designing Information.* Zurich: Lars Müller, 2014.

H

Heller, Steven. "Will Burtin's Beauty." *Print* (May 31, 2013).

Heller and Rick Landers. *Infographic Designers' Sketchbooks.* New York: Princeton Architectural Press, 2014.

Henrion, F.H.K. "A Tribute to Will Burtin." *Typographic* 1 Journal of the Society of London (1972).

I

"Information Design: Core Competencies—What Information Designers Know and Can Do." Information Design Exchange (idx), Austria: IIID Public Library, August 31, 2007. http://www.iiid.net/PublicLibrary/idx-Core-Competencies-What-information-designers-know-and-can-do.pdf

J

Jones, John Chris. *Design Methods*, 2nd ed.
New York: John Wiley, 1992.

K

Klauber, George. "Remembering Will Burtin."
Print (May 1972): 79.

Kosslyn, Steven M. *Graph Design for the Eye and Mind.*
New York: Oxford University Press, 2006.

L

Lupton, Ellen, ed. *Beautiful Users: Designing for People.*
New York: Princeton Architectural Press, 2014.

Lysen, Flora. "Blinking Brains, Corporate Spectacle and the
Atom Man: Visual Aspects of Science at the Stedelijk Museum
Amsterdam (1962)." *Stedelijk Studies* 2 (Spring 2015). http://
www.stedelijkstudies.com/journal/blinking-brains-corporate-
spectacle-and-the-atom-man/.

M

Malone, Erin K. "Robert L. Leslie." AIGA: *The Professional
Association for Design*, n.d. http://www.aiga.org/medalist-
robertleslie/. Accessed 1 April 2016.

Massey, Laura. "Fortune." *Peter Harrington London* (December
11, 2010). http://www.peterharrington.co.uk/blog/fortune/.

McKim, Robert H. *Thinking Visually: A Strategy Manual for
Problem Solving.* Belmont, CA: Lifetime Learning, 1980.

Meggs, Philip B. *A History of Graphic Design*, 3rd ed.
New York: John Wiley, 1998.

Meldrum, D.G., ed. "The Design of the Cell." *Industrial Design* 5,
no. 8 (August 1958), 56–61.

Metabolism: The Process of Life. Kalamazoo, MI:
Upjohn, 1963. Exhibition brochure. Will Burtin Papers, 74.4,
Cary Graphic Design Archive, RIT.

Miller, Paul A. *Bridging Campus and Community: Events,
Excerpts, and Expectations for Strengthening America's
Collaborative Competence: A Professional Memoir.*
Self-published, 2014.

N

Netter, Frank H. *The CIBA Collection of Medical Illustrations*
Vol. 1, *Nervous System*, 11th ed. West Caldwell, NJ: CIBA, 1975.

Norman, Don. *Living with Complexity.*
Cambridge, MA: MIT Press, 2011.

O

Okrent, Daniel. "How the World Really Works." *Fortune*
(September 19, 2005). http://archive.fortune.com/magazines/
fortune/fortune_archive/2005/09/19/8272901/index.htm.

Osborn, Alex F. *Applied Imagination: Principles and Procedures
of Creative Problem-Solving.* Rev. ed.
Buffalo, NY: Creative Education Foundation, 1993.

Owen, G. Scott. "Definitions and Rationale for Visualization."
Siggraph, 1996. https://www.cs.rit.edu/usr/local/pub/ncs/
hypervis/visgoals/visgoal2.htm.

P

Pettersson, Rune. "Information Design–Principles and
Guidelines." *Journal of Visual Literacy* 29, no. 2 (September
2010): 167–182.

Pontis, Sheila. "Guidelines for Conceptual Design to Assist
Diagram Creators in Information Design Practice." PhD diss.,
University of the Arts London, 2012.

———. *Making Sense of Field Research: A Practical Guide for
Information Designers.* Oxfordshire, UK: Routledge, 2018.

Pontis and Michael Babwahsingh. "Communicating Complexity
and Simplicity: Rediscovering the Fundamentals of Information
Design." Conference paper, 2CO–Communicating Complexity,
Sardinia, Italy, October 2013): 244–61.

Pontis and Babwahsingh. "Start with the Basics: Understanding
Before Doing." Symposium paper, IIID Vision Plus 2015,
Birmingham City University, UK, September 4, 2015),
90–102. https://www.iiid.net/downloads/IIID-VisionPlus-2015-
Proceedings.pdf.

*Position Firing Against Fighters Attacking on the Curve of
Pursuit.* US Army Air Forces Manual 20. Washington, DC: Office
of Strategic Services, May 1944. Will Burtin Papers, 64.2,
Cary Graphic Design Archive, RIT.

R

Remington, R. Roger. *Will Burtin and the Display of Visual Knowledge* Chapbook series no. 3. Rochester, NY: RIT Cary Graphic Arts Press, 2009.

Remington and Barbara Hodik. *Nine Pioneers in American Graphic Design.* Cambridge: MIT Press, 2009.

Remington and Robert S.P. Fripp. *Design and Science: The Life and Work of Will Burtin.* Hampshire, UK: Lund Humphries, 2007.

Robin, Harry. *The Scientific Image: From Cave to Computer.* New York: W.H. Freeman, 1993.

Rogers, James T. *The Pantheon Story of Mathematics for Young People.* New York: Pantheon Books, 1966.

S

Schön, Donald A. In Mary M. Kennedy, "Inexact Sciences: Professional Education and the Development of Expertise." *Review of Research in Education,* 14, no. 1 (January 1987): 133–167.

_____. *The Reflective Practitioner: How Professionals Think In Action.* New York: Basic Books, 1983.

Seelig, Tina. *inGenius: A Crash Course on Creativity.* Reprint. San Francisco: HarperOne, 2015.

Siegel, Alan and Irene Etzkorn. *Simple: Conquering the Crisis of Complexity.* New York: Twelve, 2013.

Siegel, Eric. "Too Big, Too Small, Too Slow, Too Abstract: Exhibiting Modern Science." *Exhibitionist* 27, no. 2 (Fall 2008): 22–28. https://static1.squarespace.com/static/58fa260a725e25c4f30020f3/t/59499b72f7e0abeec2b950b4/1497996195827/6+EXH_fall08_Too+Big+Too+Small+Too+Slow+Too+Abstract-Exhibiting+Modern+Science_Siegel_Baker_Martin.pdf

Sutnar, Ladislav. *Visual Design in Action.* Eds. Reto Caduff and Steven Heller, 1st ed. New York: Hastings House, 1961. Facsimile reprint, Zurich: Lars Müller, 2015.

T

Tufte, Edward R. *Beautiful Evidence.* Cheshire, CT: Graphics Press, 2006.

_____. *The Visual Display of Quantitative Information.* Cheshire, CT: Graphics Press, 1983.

_____. *Visual Explanations: Images and Quantities, Evidence and Narrative.* Cheshire, CT: Graphics Press, 1997.

V

Vignelli, Massimo. Email message to Lara Pierro de Camargo, September, 24, 2011. In "Camargo, IPD O Departamento de Design Gráfico da Cranbrook Academy of Art (1971–1995): Novos Caminhos para o Design." PhD dissertation, Universidade de São Paulo, 2012: 263.

W

Wainer, Howard. *Visual Revelations: Graphical Tales of Fate and Deception from Napoleon Bonaparte to Ross Perot.* New York: Copernicus, 1997.

Waller, Rob. "Information Design: How the Disciplines Work Together." Conference paper, Vision Plus 1, Götzis, Austria, August 1995). Reprinted as "Technical Paper 14," Reading, UK: Simplification Centre at University of Reading, 2011. https://www.robwaller.org/SC14DisciplinesTogether.pdf

Ware, Colin. *Information Visualization: Perception for Design.* Netherlands: Elsevier, 2012.

Wild, Lorraine. "Will Burtin: Design and Science." *Design Observer* (April 15, 2009), http://designobserver.com/feature/will-burtin-design-and-science/8337/.

Wurman, Richard S. "Hats." *Design Quarterly* 145 (1989): 1–32.

_____. *Information Anxiety.* New York: Doubleday, 1989.

_____. *Information Anxiety 2.* Revised ed. Indianapolis: Que, 2001.

List of Images, Diagrams and Tables

Credits

Every effort has been made to trace, clear and credit
the appropriate copyright holders of the images, diagrams
and tables reproduced in this book. However, if any credits
have been inadvertently omitted or in error, the publisher
will incorporate amendments in future printings.

Image Credits

Table of Contents, pp. xii, 2, 6, 10–18, 33–35, 68–70, 72–84, 85–87,
93, 95, 96, 120, 124–129, 142, 143
© RIT Cary Graphic Design Archive;
pp. 24–30, 44, 46, 51, 54, 57–60, 62–65, 93, 98–101, 104, 107,
109–117 © Pfizer Inc.;
pp. 40, 43, 90, 97, 147 Ezra Stoller © Esto;
p. 131 © A.V. Sobolewski;
pp. 130, 132–140 © Carol Burtin Fripp;
pp. 148–151 © Penguin Random House Inc.

Diagrams and Table Credits

pp. 20, 23, 32, 36, 37, 154 © Sheila Pontis, Ph.D., 2021.

Index

W

Winkler, Dietmar, 144
"Words in freedom," 9
World War I, 7
World War II, 3, 18, 68–87
World's Fair (New York)
        of 1939, 18
        of 1964, 126, 129
Wurman, Richard Saul, 3, 42, 105

Z

Zachary, Frank, 70
Zwart, Piet, 8

Colophon

Editor	Molly Q. Cort
Designer	Bruce Ian Meader
Typefaces	Neutraface 2 Text Book and Bold Haas Grotesk Display Black
Production	Marnie Soom
Paper	100 lb. McCoy Matte text 120 lb. Endurance Silk cover
Printing and Binding	Jostens Commercial Printing Clarksville, Tennessee